CAVE OF THE IMMORTALS

On the poet:

"Wen Tong, a genius endowed by Nature as well as a sage with innate knowledge, moved his brush as if aided by divinities to achieve subtleties in harmony with natural creation. He kept within the rules and yet roamed beyond the dusty world."

—Li Kan (1245–1320)

On the translation:

"Informed by a lifetime of scholarship, the introduction is a masterpiece of cultural history; the translations are at once scholarly, delightful, and deeply moving. To paraphrase the great Song dynasty writer Su Shi, just as Wen Tong in painting bamboo became bamboo, Jonathan Chaves in translating Wen Tong became Wen Tong."

—David K. Schneider, author of
*Confucian Prophet: Political Thought in
Du Fu's Poetry* (752–757)

CAVE OF THE IMMORTALS

The Poetry and Prose of
Bamboo Painter Wen Tong
(1019–1079)

Translated and introduced
by Jonathan Chaves

Floating World Editions

First edition, 2017
Published by Floating World Editions, Inc.
26 Jack Corner Road, Warren, CT 06777

Printed in the U.S.A.

ISBN 978-1-891640-90-2

To Tom Rimer

*When again will we face each other
beneath a brilliant moon,
Sitting as long as the pure shadows last,
discussing mysterious Zen?*

CONTENTS

Acknowledgments

It is a pleasure to acknowledge the unstinting support of my colleague, Professor Angela He Bo of Wuhan University, and especially her calling to my attention the Wanli-period edition of Wen Tong's works here used as the basic text. She also helped me to acquire a copy of the modern facsimile of this work.

Dr. Stephen Little, Curator of Chinese and Korean Art at The Los Angeles County Museum of Art, provided me with invaluable information and insight on Wen Tong's few extant paintings.

Professor Robert Gimello of the University of Notre Dame was generous in sharing with me his encyclopedic knowledge of Buddhism, and in answering definitively the questions I put to him in connection with Wen Tong's writings that delve into rarely explored regions of Buddhist practice in China.

LIST OF ILLUSTRATIONS

Front and back cover

    Wen Tong 文同 (1019–1079), *Bamboo*. Album leaf, ink on paper, 12⅛ x 19 in (31 x 48.3 cm). From the Collection of the National Palace Museum, Taipei, by permission.

p. 164 Li Kan 李衎 (1245–1320), *Bamboo and Rocks*. Pair of hanging scrolls, ink and color on silk, each 74¾ x 21¾ in (189.9 x 55.2 cm), 1318. The Metropolitan Museum of Art, image courtesy of the C.C. Wang Family, Gift of The Dillon Fund, 1973 (1973.120.7a, b).

Prose Part Title

Gu An 顧安 (ca. 1289–after 1365), *New Bamboo*. Hanging scroll, ink on paper, 35¾ x 13 in (91 x 33.1 cm), 14th century. Palace Museum, Beijing, published in the *Complete Collection of Chinese Painting (Zhongguo huihua quanji)*, vol. 8 (Beijing: Wenwu chubanshe, 1999).

p. 215 *Six-Armed, Eleven-Headed Guanyin*. Cloth banner, ink and color on silk, painting proper 39³⁄₁₆ x 24¾ in (99.6 x W. 62.8 cm). Reportedly retrieved from Dunhuang, Gansu Province, China, dated 985. Harvard Art Museums/Arthur M. Sackler Museum, Bequest of Grenville L. Winthrop, 1943.57.14.

p. 230 Grave mound of Wen Tong, Yongtaixiang, Yanting County, Sichuan, China.

INTRODUCTION

When Yü-k'o painted bamboo,
He saw bamboo only, never people.
Did I say he saw no people?
So rapt he forgot even himself—
He himself became bamboo,
Putting out fresh growth endlessly.
Chuang Tzu no longer with us,
Who can fathom this uncanny power?[1]

—Su Shi

Rarely in history has such transcendent praise been showered upon an artist by a contemporary fellow-artist of the stature of Su Shi (also Su Dongpo, 1037–1101). Su, himself one of the giants of Chinese poetry, one of the greatest calligraphers of his day and a painter who occasionally did bamboo paintings, was easily the leading cultural arbiter of his generation, a foundational figure in the history of Chinese literature and art. Wen Tong (or Wen T'ung 文同, 1019–1079), style name Yuke (or Yü-k'o 與可), his elder by eighteen years and in fact a distant cousin, being thus recognized for his brilliance as a painter specializing in bamboo—although he did other subjects as well—became for centuries the single most famous artist to work on this theme, and as such he remains known today. Li Kan (1245–1320), one of the major bamboo painters of the subsequent Yuan dynasty (1279–1368), when bamboo painting would become fully established as a genre among literati artists, wrote a *Zhu pu*, or *Manual of Bamboo [Painting]*, in which he stated:

Only Wen Tong, a genius endowed by Nature, as well as a sage with innate knowledge, moved his brush as if aided by divinities

---

1 Burton Watson, *Su Tung-p'o: Selections from a Sung Dynasty Poet* (New York: Columbia University Press, 1965; reprinted Copper Canyon Press, 1993), p. 107.

to achieve subtleties in harmony with natural creation. He kept within the rules and yet roamed beyond the dusty world.[2]

Wen Tong of course did not *invent* the bamboo theme, nor was he the first great master of the genre; that honor apparently belongs to a certain Xiao Yue of the Tang dynasty (618–906), whose works have long since disappeared. Xiao's reputation is founded upon a great poem by Bai Juyi (also Po Chü-i, 772–846), "Song of Painting Bamboo":

> Of all the plants, bamboo is hardest to depict—
> Although past and present, some have painted it,
>   none have even come close.
> Intendant Xiao alone in applying his brush
>   has touched the true image;
> In the entire history of the art,
>   he is the only one!
> Others have shown the bamboo's body
>   as bulging, fat;
> Xiao pictures the stalks as slender,
>   up-thrusting, knot by knot.
> Others have shown the bamboo's branches
>   dead, sickly hanging there;
> Xiao pictures the branches alive,
>   each single leaf in motion . . .[3]

With Xiao's works gone, and no bamboo paintings of the Tang dynasty extant, we are dependent on Bai's "word-painting" for some hint of what bamboo painting may have been like prior to Wen Tong. But with Wen, it is fair to say, the art was reborn and given its characteristic calligraphic sweep and power.

But as early as the late twelfth century, in 1195, when the relatively obscure scholar Jia Chengzhi—a Sichuan man who served as Magistrate of Qiongzhou in Sichuan just as Wen Tong had done for a

---

2   Translated by Susan Bush and Hsio-yen Shih, from their *Early Chinese Texts on Painting* (Harvard University Press, 1985), p. 278. See pp. 275–280 *passim* for Wen Tong's importance to later bamboo masters.

3   Bai Juyi (also Bai Xiangshan), *Bai Xiangshan shiji (The Collected Poetry of Bai Xiangshan)*, edition of the *Sibu beiyao*, 12/6a. Unless otherwise noted, all translations are by the author.

Bamboo by a Stream Bank, Hu Zao (fl.1646–87). Album leaf, ink and color on paper, 9 ¼ x 12 ⅜ in (23.5 x 31.4 cm). Courtesy of the Tsao Family Collection of Seventeenth Century Chinese Painting. Photograph by Michael Tropea. The artist names Wen Tong as the first major bamboo painter.

period—published the edition of Wen Tong's writings that would become the basis for later reprintings, he lamented that:

> People know Huzhou's [Wen Tong's] painting, but they have not yet learned how to love his literary writings! It is not that his writings are lacking in the skillfulness of his painting, but rather that people have not had sufficient access to them. The extraordinary brilliance of his painting originally *derived from* the energy left over after he had worked on his writings; and the noble spirit of antiquity in his writings *derives from* the basic essence within his heart.[4]

---

4   Jia Chengzhi, colophon to the collected works of Wen Tong. This will be found in the basic text for the current book, *Xinke Shishi Xiansheng Danyuanji* (*The Newly [Re] printed Collection from the Abyss of the Elixir by Master Stone House, preface dated 1612*); *Xubian zhugong shuhan shiwen* (*Additional selection of letters, poems and prose writings [about or to Wen Tong] by various gentlemen*), pp. 28a–29a (pp. 345–346); and *Anthology* (see note 6 below), pp. 212–213. The colophon is dated 1195.

Jia continues to note that Su Shi himself and his beloved younger broth-
er, friend, and fellow poet, Su Zhe (also Su Che, or Su Ch'e, 1039–1112)
were great admirers of Wen's literary works, as well as of his painting.

Thus, even in China, where the phenomenon of painters who were
also fine poets is widespread,[5] accomplishments in one art can obscure
those in another. In the hope of correcting this unjustified neglect, the
present collection of translations of Wen Tong's poetry, with some of his
prose, is offered.[6]

1

Wen Tong, like Su Shi, was a man of Sichuan, born in 1019 in Zitong
county, present-day Yantingxian. His career, of course, was that of a
scholar-official in the administrative system, based as it was upon the
civil service examination. Wen earned his *jinshi*, "presented scholar" de-
gree in 1049 at the age of thirty-two (Chinese count, taking into ac-
count the discrepancy between the lunar and solar calendars, as well as
reckoning the person to be one year old at birth). He then embarked
upon the usual series of official positions, but unlike Su Shi, he would
spend almost the whole of his career in his home province of Sichuan,
and the relatively nearby southwestern part of Shaanxi Province, return-
ing to his hometown twice for the mandated periods of mourning for
his father and mother (three years, sometimes reduced to two years and
three months). For his father's death, Wen Tong returned for a period
during the years 1061–63; for his mother's, 1067–69. He did have three
relatively brief stints in the Northern Song capital Bianjing, or Bianliang
(today's Kaifeng), but on the whole his career was unusual in dispatching
him to remoter parts of China, places rarely administered by well-known
scholar-officials.

---

5   For the poetry-painting relationship in China, see Jonathan Chaves, *The Chinese
Painter as Poet* (New York: China Institute in America, 2000).
6   In 1985, the Sichuan Arts and Letters Publishing House (Sichuan wen'yi chu-
banshe) in Chengdu published the sole modern anthology of Wen Tong's poetry, *Wen
Tong shi xuan (An Anthology of Selected Poems by Wen Tong*, hereafter *Anthology)*, edited by
He Zengluan and Liu Taiyan. This fine work is an example of the welcome return of the
mainland Chinese publishing world to classical literature in the 1980s, after the suspen-
sion of virtually all such publication activity during the disastrous "Cultural Revolution"
of 1966–76. I have made extensive use of this book in preparing the present volume. See
Bibliographical Note, p. 33.

Ironically, the place name which would attach itself to his surname, in accordance with a practice by which the name of a official's place of service became a kind of alternate cognomen, was Huzhou 湖州, located to the southwest of Taihu (Great Lake) near Suzhou in the southeastern part of China, to the magistracy of which Wen was indeed named at the very end of his life. But he was to die in 1079 en route from the capital to this place, without ever having served there.

Wen was very proud of his Sichuan roots, and identified strongly with the region. For example, in his prose *An Account of the Paintings of Master Zhang of Pengzhou*, he writes of the rich legacy of Buddhist art in Sichuan, anticipating by centuries the modern interest in concentrating on regional characteristics in cultural history:[7]

> Sichuan has been a place of many outstanding craftsmen, ever since the two emperors of Tang [i.e., Tang Xuanzong, or Minghuang, and his son, later to become Emperor Suzong] took refuge in Sichuan [after 755] and brought as part of their entourage Imperial Painting Intendants.
>
> Therefore, preserved in the temple precincts of all the various districts of Chengdu and environs are images of Buddhas, Bodhisattvas, Luohans, etc., of such a number that other places in the world, although they certainly can be said to possess many ancient remains, are not as rich in this type of art as is this region.

Wen spends so much time in his poetry expressing his delight at getting away from official duties, and withdrawing to the serenity of the nearby gardens (sometimes part of the official headquarters), that we will honor and emulate his example by avoiding a detailed account of each office and title he held. It should be noted, however, as did Fan Bailu (1030–1094), the author of Wen's *muzhiming* or "tomb epitaph,"[8] that Wen earned a reputation as an "uncorrupt official," who took the sufferings of the people to heart. For example, Fan records that when he was appointed to the magistracy of Lingzhou in Sichuan, in 1070:

> . . . Wen personally visited the people when they were sick or suffering. Upon discovering that there were gangs in the city who paid

---

7   See *Xinke* . . . (hereafter *DYJ*), 22/6b–7a.
8   In *Anthology*, pp. 207–211.

no heed to authority, and every night would perpetrate outrages against those on the roads, so that law-abiding citizens at night would lock their doors and not dare to come out, Wen arrested them on some pretext, brought them to his office, and put severe restrictions on them, warning them, "Never again disrupt my region!" After this, the people came and went for all affairs, whether happy or lamentable, and they would travel at night carrying lanterns, no one ever again daring to bother them. At the time of the joyous celebrations of the Lantern Festival, the country folk, propping up the elderly and holding the children by the hand would come all the way to the city, and everything was entirely peaceful.

A group of men from Guiping, however, on the pretext of distributing "divine gifts," deluded people with demonic arts, attracting people from far and near, all of whom paid them large amounts in cash or goods, thus promoting wasteful extravagance in various shrines. Wen heard of this, and sent agents to arrest the leaders. These he had branded and exiled, paying no attention to their followers . . . The local people regarded him as a divinity.

Fan Bailu also presents Wen Tong as a magistrate who brought education and culture to the regions he governed, considered to be a major obligation of the true Confucian scholar-official. When he was appointed to govern Xingyuan on the Han River (1073–75), according to Fan:

Wen found that the Han River valley was rich and fruitful, but in customs the region, however prosperous, was lacking in cultivation, and had produced no *jinshi* degree holders. His Excellency [Wen] first put the local academies in order, and selected the best of the young scholars to run these. He spread a cultured atmosphere throughout the region, causing the people to send their sons and younger brothers to school.

On his own days of leisure, he would personally visit the academies to observe them, himself taking over the instructor's role. With this, the culture of the region improved, with the great emphasis being on learning. Here too there were thieves infesting the marketplace. His Excellency had them arrested and interrogated, and they all kowtowed to him and confessed . . .

Fan goes on to relate how Wen remitted onerous taxation, and later when appointed to govern at Yangzhou (in Shaanxi, not to be confused with the city in southeastern China, written with a different character), reformed the tea trade to the advantage of the local people. In every respect, then, Wen was regarded as a model Confucian magistrate, concerned for the welfare of the citizenry.

Wen's concern is reflected in his poetry. Although he did not produce a large number of "social" poems comparable to Bai Juyi's famous series of fifty New Music Bureau poems, Wen is able to give us a window into the stark reality of everyday lives among some of the poorest of his constituents:

The Water Mill [9]

Where water rushes, they made a water mill,
    the people of Jialing;
Canal walls tall, bottom deep,
    grueling is the labor!
Within a radius of three and a third miles
    everyone shares this mill:
Wheat in, flour out,
    so nobody will do without.
But the workers here live in dangerous spots,
    what they can produce is meager;
For generations they've fed the folks
    who live along the river.
Oh, may the Court see fit to send an investigator,
    to improve this use of water power:
Please have pity on these straight-wheeled
    and slant-wheeled carts.

The poet's brief is apparently for easing the lives of the laborers, who are tasked with maintaining this heavily utilized facility in an area difficult of access, as well as carting in and out the wheat and flour on dangerous slopes, where they must live as well to maintain the schedule of the work. If an Imperial inspector or investigator reported truthfully on the situation, perhaps something might be done to alleviate their distress.

---

9   *DYJ*, 17/6a.

The poem could almost be a formal memorial to the throne, except that Wen is writing as a poet after all in this piece, deflecting the court's and the reader's pity to the two types of *carts* used by the locals, which become a kind of kenning for the people themselves.

2

As a poet, Wen was admired in his own day by Su Shi, as we have noted, but with very few exceptions scholars in later dynasties were unaware of his poetry. During the Ming dynasty (1368–1644), poetry of the Song (960–1279) in general was forgotten, or in some cases denigrated as inferior to that of the Tang. The poetry in question was, of course, the *shi* 詩, a form with the same number of characters per line—usually five or seven—and following elaborate rules of prosody, rhyme, and tonal euphony. In modern times, the genre known as *ci* 詞, with uneven line lengths, which indeed flourished in the Song, has risen to prominence among specialists in Chinese literature, and has regained some degree of popularity among younger Chinese readers who love poetry. But the *ci* was never regarded as equal in importance and *gravitas* to the *shi* among traditional scholars. Wen Tong appears not to have written in this genre.

Late in the Ming, there began a revival of interest in Song *shi* poetry, which reached full bloom in the early Qing with the publication of such important works as *Song shi jishi (Recording Matters Pertaining to Song Shi Poetry)* compiled by Li E (1692–1752), which has a section on Wen Tong, and the magisterial collectanea of literary anthologies, the *Song shi chao (Volumes of Song Shi Poetry)* edited by Wu Zhizhen (1640–1717), *et al.* The latter includes a generous anthology of Wen Tong's poems, and a later addendum of the nineteenth century provides many more.

Wen Tong as it happens was idiosyncratically recognized as a poet in the mid-Ming by Yang Shen (1488–1559), a poet, antiquarian, and a scholarly polymath with an extraordinary range of interests.[10] In his ex-

---

10   For Yang Shen, see L. Carrrington Goodrich and Chaoying Fang, *Dictionary of Ming Biography* (New York and London: Columbia University Press, 1976), Vol. 2, pp. 1531–1535. For selections of his poetry, see Jonathan Chaves, *The Columbia Book of Later Chinese Poetry* (New York: Columbia University Press, 1976), see pp. 267–280. For his antiquarian activities, and another of his most important poems, see the same author's "Still Hidden by Spirits and Immortals: The Quest for the Elusive 'Stele of Yu the Great,'" *Asia Major*, Third Series, Vol. XXVI, Part I, 2013, pp. 1–22.

tensive *Sheng'an shihua (Comments on Poetry from the Ascension Studio)*,[11] Yang notes that:

> Dongpo [Su Shi] fulsomely praised Wen Yuke's poetry, and yet it has rarely been transmitted in the world. I happen to have a copy of the *Danyuan ji* [Wen's collected works] in my home, and his five-character per line regulated verse poems have the flavor of Wei Suzhou and Meng Xiangyang [two major Tang poets; see below]. True it is that Master Dongpo did not heap empty accolades upon them. At this time, I will record several of them here . . .

With this, Yang records eight of Wen Tong's poems in full,[12] apparently assuming his readers would not have had easy access to them. And he finishes with this telling remark:

> If one were to place these eight poems in the collected works of the various masters of the Kaiyuan [713–41] period, readers would almost be incapable of distinguishing the difference! When people today say, "The Song dynasty had no poetry!"—how could they possibly be right?

Yang Shen here is almost single-handedly rehabilitating Song dynasty poetry at a time when the orthodox view held that the High Tang period, i.e., the Kaiyuan period—that of Du Fu (712–72) Li Bai (also Li Po, 701–762), Wang Wei (699–759), and Meng Haoran (Xiangyang, 689/691–740), to name only the four most famous— represented the ultimate in poetic achievement, and everything thereafter represented a falling off of literary quality. Yang states that Wen at his best is on the same level as these giants, and he even considers his style to be reminiscent of that of Meng Haoran and Wei Yingwu (Suzhou, 737–92), another major poet of the period. He here calls attention to the quiet vignettes of nature, usually as experienced by a solitary poet, that are characteristic of Meng in particular, as well as of Wang Wei. This is supreme praise.

---

11   See the edition of *Xu Lidai shihua (Continuation of "Comments-on-poetry" Texts Down through the Eras)*, reprint in five volumes of 1915 publication, ed. by Ding Fubao (Taipei: Yiwen yinshuguan), Vol. 1, 1/11a–b. See also *Anthology*, p. 35.
12   Poems 15, 23, 24, and 90 of this book are included by Yang among the eight.

In the West, only a handful of Wen's poems have appeared. Launcelot Cranmer-Byng (1872–1945) deserves credit for including, remarkably, two poems (actually one split into two) by Wen in his book *A Feast of Lanterns* of 1916.[13] The redoubtable Robert Van Gulik (1910–67), in his delightful study of gibbons and gibbon-lore in China, included a full translation of Wen's lengthy lament for the death of a pet gibbon, as well as another poem on gibbons.[14] I myself added three more of Wen's poems in a literary magazine, *The G. W. Review*, in 1989.[15] These last are included in the present volume.

The early Qing scholars who rediscovered Song poetry recognized that it possessed characteristics that differentiated it from most Tang poetry. In a word, we may say the Song poets were moving in the direction of understated *realism*, faithful to the details of everyday life.[16] Wen's poem on the water mill (see above) would be a good example.

A particular achievement of Wen in poetry consists of sequences of quatrains, often rather long, on garden-estates. Here his feeling for nature and man's place in it is orchestrated to the full. For example, in one series of no less than thirty poems, "Miscellaneous Poems on the Gardens and Ponds of Defense Residence" (see poems 197–226), Wen demonstrates what appears to be an infinite capacity for ringing variations on the theme of man-in-nature. In the very first poem, "Lake Bridge," he writes:

> Flying bridge spanning Crosswise Lake:
> Lying there, just like a giant rainbow.
> I ask: "Within a single day,
> How many people cross over you, back and forth?"

The conceit of a dialogue between the poet and the bridge is unusual in Chinese poetry, where personification is relatively rare. But at the same time, such a quatrain as this, with its charmingly unexpected finish

---

13   Launcelot Cranmer-Byng, *A Feast of Lanterns* (London: John Murray, 1916), p. 79. The two, entitled "Morning" and "Evening" respectively, appear to be based upon the two halves of poem 25 here, "Living in a Village."

14   Robert Van Gulik, *The Gibbon in China: An Essay in Chinese Animal Lore* (Leiden: E. J. Brill, 1967), pp. 77–78. I am grateful to Stephen Addiss for calling these examples to my attention.

15   *The G. W. Review*, Vol. 9, No. 2 (1989), pp. 14–15.

16   For a superb presentation of the whole subject, see Burton Watson, trans., Yoshikawa Kōjirō, *An Introduction to Sung Poetry* (Harvard University Press, 1967).

anticipates the development of the type in such Southern Song poets as Yang Wanli (1127–1206) or Fan Chengda (1126–1193).[17]

Wen does not, however, by any means limit himself to the miniature, however evocative. His long poem on the kingfisher (280), for example, goes into considerable detail, based on careful observation:

> Suddenly—a plunge into the clear ripples:
> He's snatched some tidbit the size of a needle-point;
> He does the same again, some three times, or four,
> Then, satiated, he's full right to the throat!
> Replete and satisfied,
> He takes wing, returning to his old pond,
> Flying, calling to his beloved mate,
> And her cry is heard, harmonizing chime-like with his.

The expansion of Wen's horizons, however, is really apparent in his many poems that deal with the realm of the Immortals, and the Daoistic, alchemical search for an Elixir of Immortality. In poem 148, he describes how he purchases some putative elixir:

> I therefore purchased some, not sparing any cash,
> And, following the instructions, imbibed the herb
>   going on two years now.
> The effectiveness has been divinely sagely,
>   felt now only after this long a time:
> Sinews strong, body overflowing with energy,
>   limbs and joints all powerful.
> I ask myself, when will I be able to ascend
>   to that Cinnabar Empyrean,
> So I can, soon as possible, grow two wings,
>   and thus to soar up high?
> In am like a prisoner in this realm of dust,
>   and can live here no longer:
> I await the sight of Great Vastness,
>   where I'll join Cloud Generals!

---

17 For Yang, see Jonathan Chaves, *Heaven My Blanket, Earth My Pillow: Poems from Sung-Dynasty China by Yang Wan-li* (New York and Tokyo: Weatherhill, 1976); for Fan, see J. D. Schmidt, *Stone Lake: The Poetry of Fan Chengda* (Cambridge University Press, 1992).

One's imagination can scarcely soar any higher. When modern man flies in rocket-propelled vessels into space, he is attempting in his literal fashion to fulfill age-old and universal dreams of ascension, beyond this "realm of dust." If Wen Tong could visit Cape Kennedy, he would be surprised by the technology, but not by the vision driving it. If anything, given the determined secularism of the modern mind, Wen's imagination aims beyond "space" itself. In fact, in addition to the Confucian aspect of his life that we have already seen in his official career, Wen engaged with other religious traditions of his day, Daoism as a practiced religion, and especially Buddhism. And beyond even these, the "Three Teachings" (*san jiao*) of Chinese civilization, there are elements of eclectic Chinese folk religion echoed in his writings.

3

One of China's great contributions to literature has been a body of ekphrastic poetry without parallel, with Bai Juyi's poem on a bamboo painter of the Tang dynasty an excellent example. As a poet particularly interested in painting, Wen Tong gives us a unique set of no less than twenty poems on the subject, entitled "Miscellaneous Poems on the Repository of Painting" (292–311), while many other examples are scattered throughout his collected works. The painters who have inspired him range from names today recognized as giants, to others unknown to us. It becomes clear, in any case, that Wen's love for painting is much more than that of an "art lover;" he sees the world itself in terms of the painter's vision, as in poem 191:

> Peaks and ridges—just like a Li Cheng!
> Streams and valleys—Fan Kuan alone could do them.

Li Cheng (919–967) and Fan Kuan (fl. 990–1020), two supreme masters of Chinese painting, here inform the poet's way of viewing nature. Nature and Art, in Chinese cosmological thinking, share the same roots in the underlying patternings of the cosmos. The poet may move from painting to nature, or from nature to painting. Again, from poem 192:

> If you, sir, wish to comprehend
>   the painting of Yingqiu [Li Cheng],

Just take a look, there, in the east,
  fifth layer from the ground.

When the poet's attention turns to a contemporary, he gives us this example of versified art history, ninth in the series "Repository of Painting" (292–311):

Cold Forest by Xu Daoning

Mr. Xu may have emulated Li Yingqiu,
But his ink-path, freely wandering,
  emerges from himself!
Intersecting branches, light and agile,
  like Pei Min's "Dance of the Sword!"
Wild vines, so fluent, free,
  like Zhang Xiao's calligraphy.

Xu Daoning (also Hsü Tao-ning, ca. 970–1051/53), is today recognized as one of the great Northern Song masters. Wen clearly spots his genius, saying that even though he worked in the manner of the great Li Cheng (Yingqiu), he developed his own style. This is high praise indeed.

The second couplet concentrates on the brilliance of his brushwork, always a prime concern in Chinese connoisseurship. The painter's brushwork is ultimately seen as deriving from calligraphic strokes. Pei Min's sword dance, especially the movement of his sword tip in the air, like that of a calligrapher's brush, could inspire artists. Zhang Xiao was presumably a famed calligrapher, also of the Tang dynasty. The close link between painting and calligraphy—both executed by the same type of brush, both based on the same fundamental brush-strokes, was a given in Chinese art theory.

It will be noted that Wen Tong here leaps beyond artistic lineage, as important as that always was in China: he lets us know that Xu Daoning's art "emerges from himself." Such a claim would not seem bold in the Romantic era of the West, when the artist's or the poet's creativity was indeed seen in this manner by hypothesis; but in the Chinese context this is a big statement. Recently, Katharine Burnett has argued for the elevation of *originality*, explicitly articulated, in late Ming to early Qing thought (the seventeenth century);[18] here, that development is anticipated in Wen Tong's evaluation of Xu Daoning's achievement.

Nor is Wen Tong's idea limited to this one poem. Elsewhere (poem 82), in extolling a painting of a noble crane by an unidentified artist called only Young Li, he waxes enthusiastic:

Young Li Paints a Crane

Dignified, noble—Bluefield Mountain stock;
Mystic grandeur, here on the plain silk.
Whole body charged with ten-thousand mile yearning,
Eyes fixed on the ninefold Empyrean.
Razor sharp, the quills of displayed feathers;
Statuesque, bone-structure in full view.
And from whom, sir, did you ever learn this art?
No, it must have been intuition divine!
You received it beyond imagined forms,
You show it where your splendid brush sets down.
Xue Ji? Huang Quan?—should these masters return to life,
You'd contest with them who really is supreme!

Young Li has been divinely inspired, again, an idea that might be thought "Romantic," unless we wish to see an echo, much closer in date, of medieval European ideas of a more strictly religious inspiration at work in the selfless illuminators of manuscripts and sculptors of church and cathedral reliefs and statues. (Even here, we should remember the personal pride expressed by such artists as Gislebertus [fl. ca. 1125] at Autun—signing his great Tympanum "*Gislebertus hoc fecit*"—"Gislebertus made this.")[19] The idea that "moderns" can actually *surpass* the ancients—here Xue Ji (649–713) and Huang Quan (903–965), two famous masters of "bird-and-flower" painting—in certain branches of painting is a new one, characteristic of the eleventh century.[20]

---

18   Katharine Burnett, *Dimensions of Originality: Essays on Seventeenth-Century Chinese Art Theory and Criticism* (Hong Kong: The Chinese University Press, 2013).

19   See Dennis Grivot, *Twelfth Century Sculpture in the Cathedral of Autun* (S.A.E.P. Colmar-Ingersheim, 1980), p. 1 and *passim*.

20   For this, see Jonathan Chaves, *Mei Yao-ch'en and the Development of Early Sung Poetry* (New York: Columbia University Press, 1976), pp. 202–204.

Although we do know that Wen Tong painted landscapes, includ-
ing one lost work inspired by the great Tang dynasty thinker, Han Yu's
(768–824) prose preface and poem, "Seeing Off Li Yuan on his Retire-
ment to Pangu,"[21] which conjures up an Arcadian paradise to which Li is
understood to be retiring, Wen's primary subject was, of course, bamboo.
In "Ink-Lord Hall" (poem 50) he himself tells us:

> I love bamboo! I plant it and I paint it!
> —As if surrounded by beams of a kingly palace!
> Within the high hall, they lean against a remote cliff,
> On whitewashed walls, crisscrossing their spreading branches.
> Their mountain shadows shade autumn serenity;
> Their moon colors purify nighttime's void.
> This austere elegance—only I enjoy it:
> Who else can love this retreat of mine?

This is only one of a great many delightful poems on bamboo—real or
painted, or both. Wen Tong, again in accordance with the "realism" we
have noted in Song poetry as a whole, lets us know that not only does he
paint bamboo, he actually plants it as well, so that he can live in proxim-
ity to this noblest of all flora.

One might say that the meanings (e.g., "austere elegance") thus far at-
tributed to bamboo by Wen Tong are Confucian; but the most extensive
and original of his bamboo poems (193) unexpectedly gives a particularly
Chan Buddhist meaning to the plant: the recipient of its title, "Sent to
be Inscribed on the Bamboo Studio of Master Ze of Kaiyuan Temple," is
specifically a Chan master, a Buddhist monk. The first eight lines of this
twenty-line poem tell us:

> Master Ze's been planting bamboo,
>   for thirty years so far,
> The bamboo grown, filling the courtyard,
>   breathing out green mist.

---

21   See Jonathan Chaves, "'Traces Buried among the Market Towns': Literary Expres-
sions of Reclusion," in Peter C. Sturman and Susan S. Tai, eds., *The Artful Recluse; Paint-
ing, Poetry, and Politics in Seventeenth-Century China* (Santa Barbara Museum of Art and
DelMonico Books-Prestel, 2012), p. 64.

These blue-green dragon-sons and grandsons
  so flourishing and full,
Their ancestry must be traced back
  to Wei River valley.
Absorbing wind and storing rain,
  shading the walls of the hall,
No one dares approach them lightly,
  so cold and dignified!
Their fragrance always enters in
  among the Buddha-thrones;
Their leaves fall, but don't reach as far
  as *sutra*-window seats.

It is almost as if the bamboo is *participating* in the Master's worship of the various Buddhas whose icons adorn the temple-monastery where he resides, and is striving to reach out to the pages of the sacred texts that have been brought near the window so as to afford illumination for reading. The *coldness* of the bamboo is a positive quality; here the Confucian ideas of loyalty and trustworthiness (the bamboo flourishes, green, even in the cold; coldness itself often suggests unsoiled purity) are conjoined with Buddhist devotion.

Closely related to ekphrastic poetry are poems on archaeological objects, a sub-genre that flourishes for the first time in the Northern Song. Han Yu and his contemporaries did initiate the type with their poems on the then newly discovered "Stone Drums," round, "drum"-shaped stone monuments with inscriptions from the Zhou dynasty (today dated to the fifth century BC). But, as Richard Rudolph showed in an important article of 1963,[22] a particular interest in antiquity as reflected in archaeological objects is characteristic of the Northern Song dynasty. It was Ouyang Xiu (also Hsiu, 1007–1072), in fact, who compiled the first archaeological catalogue of sorts—a chronologically arranged annotated list of epigraphical inscriptions from stone monuments and bronze vessels and other objects; called the *Jigu lu (A Record of Gathered Antiquities)*, it is included in his collected works. Ouyang's great friend and one of the major poets of the eleventh century, Mei Yaochen (1002–1060), developed Han Yu's "Stone Drums" concept into a full-fledged sub-genre with numerous

---

22   Richard Rudolph, "Preliminary Notes on Sung Archaeology," *Journal of Asian Studies*, Vol. 22 (1963), pp. 169–177.

important poems on such objects. Friends in turn with both men was probably the leading private collector of bronze vessels and other artifacts, and a fine poet as well, Liu Chang (Yuanfu, 1019–1068). Mei spent many enjoyable times at Liu's house, viewing his collection and writing poems about different items in it.[23]

In these poems, the authors would engage in Confucian historiography, that is, what is known as "praise-and-blame" (*baobian*, 褒貶). This concept is associated with none other than Confucius (551–479 BC) himself, as he employed it in the one classic text whose authorship is actually attributed to him, the *Chun qiu (Spring and Autumn Annals)*, a date-by-date history of his home state of Lu over a certain period of time. The historian is seen as a moral adjudicator, laying out the actions of a key figure, and then judging whether he acted morally or not, or, in certain cases, in a morally ambiguous manner. Sima Qian (ca.135–86 BC) adopted this approach, giving his judgments at the end of each biography in his section of biographical accounts in his *Shi ji (Records of the Historian)*.

In his poems of this type Wen also delivers judgments on the actions of historical figures. But there is a perhaps uneasy balance between

Lü Wancun's Ink Bamboo, Lü Liuliang (1629–1683). Hanging scroll, ink on paper, 28¾ x 14½ in (73 x 37 cm). Image courtesy of the Paul Moss collection, UK.

---

23   For all of this, see Jonathan Chaves, *Mei Yao-ch'en . . .*, pp. 210 ff.

this strand and an unmistakable attraction on the poet's part towards the aesthetic excellence of the calligraphy, for example, exhibited in the works. That is to say, despite the general view in Confucian thought that the *Good* and the *Beautiful* go together—only a good man can create a truly great work of art—Wen runs up against the problem that a man he considers manifestly *bad* can be the patron at least of a calligraphic masterpiece. This problem emerges with crystal clarity in poem 287, "A Proclamation of the Qin Dynasty." The text of the proclamation is incised upon the surface of a weight dated precisely to the year 209 BC, during the brief reign of the son of the founder of this historically important but very short dynasty. "The text is crisp and simple," Wen states, "The calligraphy strokes are wonderfully fine." But Wen feels what any literatus of conscience would feel about the second emperor of the Qin, whose proclamation calls for the title of his father, Qin Shi Huangdi, to be properly included on all weights and measures: he (Wen) despises the Qin, which was anti-Confucian in that the first Qin emperor famously "burned the books" (the Confucian classics, except for the *Yi jing*, or *Book of Changes*) and "buried the scholars" (the *ru*, Confucian scholars who were masters of these classical texts and who based their philosophy upon them). The Qin was founded upon the so-called Fajia, or Legalist School, as it is usually and misleadingly translated; School of Policy might be a better rendition. While the Confucian School (Rujia, or School of the Ru Scholars) considered the *moral character and charisma* of the ruler to be all-important, the policy thinkers, Machiavellian *avant la lettre* perhaps, or even like modern "policy wonks," regarded moral character as irrelevant, and the specific *measures* enacted to be key.

And so, immediately after praising the calligraphy on the object, Wen bursts out with this:

> But, Hai! What kind of man were you,
> To dare to become a joke for ten thousand generations?
> What you did was simply not right!
> This might serve as a mere spirit-tablet.
> So petty-minded, calling for eulogies of what is trivial!
> Looking back, it's all lamentable! . . .

This is intensely felt. To begin with, Wen addresses the second Qin emperor by his "civilian" personal name, Hai, implying that he was no emperor at all, a serious insult. And he thinks the proclamation is an entirely inappropriate text, calling for the glorification of the short-lived and cruel dynasty and its founder.

The combination of aesthetic appreciation and historiographical condemnation is unusual and refreshingly human in its apparent incoherence.

4

It is by now apparent that Confucianism, Buddhism, and Daoism are all amply represented in Wen Tong's poetry. Friendship between scholar-officials and Buddhist monks—with the former developing serious interest in reading Buddhist *sutras*, and in the actual practice of Buddhism, while the latter write classical poetry, by no means necessarily on specifically Buddhist themes—reaches a kind of height in the Northern Song dynasty, as Robert Gimello has shown in a seminal article.[24] The depth of Wen Tong's relationship with one particular Buddhist monk, Minxing, also Wuyan,[25] is apparent from his prose preface (no. 8) and poem 131 on "seeing him off" from the capital as the monk returns to Chengdu. In the prose account, Wen starts by describing how enamored he was of the great Daoist philosopher Zhuangzi (fourth century BC), prior to meeting Minxing. Even before this important event, the writings of one of the most important monks in the history of Chinese Buddhism, Sengzhao[26] (384–418), had such an impact upon him that he underwent what was in effect a conversion. (Paradoxically, on perhaps a deeper level, the "equal" status of the Three Teachings could co-exist with a revulsion against one and in favor of another, i.e., conversion[27]):

---

24   Robert Gimello, "Mārga and Culture: Learning, Letters, and Liberation in Northern Sung Ch'an," in Robert E. Buswell, Jr. and Robert M. Gimello, eds., *Paths to Liberation: the Mārga and its Transformations in Buddhist Thought* (University of Hawaii Press, 1992).

25   For Minxing, see Chang Bide, *et al, Songren zhuanji ziliao suoyin* (*An Index to Biographical Materials on People of the Song Dynasty*), in six volumes (Taipei: Dingwen shuju, 1975), Vol. 5, p. 4433.

26   He is described by Arthur F. Wright as the author of "one of the most important Chinese Buddhist texts," which includes his "discussions," referred to by Wen Tong elsewhere in his prose preface, on such matters as "things not changing" (because their being is so tenuous that there really is nothing there to change), and "things not truly existing." See *Buddhism in Chinese History* (Stanford University Press, 1959), p. 135. Sengzhao's master was the greatest of translators of Buddhist texts from Sanskrit into Chinese, Kumārajīva (343/344–413).

27   For more on this, see Jonathan Chaves, *Singing of the Source: Nature and God in the Poetry of the Chinese Painter, Wu Li (1638–1712),* (University of Hawaii Press, 1993), ch. 2.

When I now looked back at the doctrines of "free-and-easy wandering," and "the relativity of all things," which previously I had admired, oh, how petty and contentious they now seemed. And as for their having heights that could never be trod, and depths that could never be plummeted [i.e., Zhuangzi's ideas seemed merely fantastical], I now took the liberty of considering these to be disastrous flaws.

And then Minxing appeared, and

. . . for me he established the Ladder to the Extinction of Karma, and extended the Rope that Extirpates Fallacies, enabling me to relax and free myself, to call upon the Non-Ultimate, and to reach the point where within the time of a single breath, Void and Form would all disappear. So great has been the power of Wuyan's [Minxing's] influence upon me. And what level of gift can one say this is that I have thus received from him?

It might be noted that Minxing, in addition to being a charismatic teacher of Buddhism, was a painter of Luohan, or Buddhist saints, and other Buddhist subjects, recorded as such in the authoritative source *Tuhui baojian (The Precious Mirror of Painting)*, dating from the fourteenth century.[28] In another prose text (no. 5), Wen Tong discusses the tradition of Buddhist art in Sichuan, and states that Minxing was descended from a certain "Master Zhang" (Minxing's secular surname would thus have been Zhang) who was an outstanding painter of Buddhist subjects: "Minxing is outstandingly brilliant and comprehensively knowledgeable, and is himself expert at this art!"

In seriously taking Minxing as his master in Chan Buddhism, Wen Tong was already going beyond what might be called the norm for such relationships. But a truly extraordinary component of Wen's involvement in Buddhism is his interest in the esoteric type of Buddhist religion (Mijiao, or "secret teaching"). This is particularly apparent in his intriguing prose essay "An Account of a Divine Dream" (no. 7). Here we learn of a lady, wife of a military official, who is said to have been pregnant but unable to deliver for five years, beginning in the year 1070. She dreams

---

28   See the edition of *Meishu congkan (Collectanea of the Fine Arts)* in four volumes (Taipei, 1956+), Vol. 2 (1964), p. 179.

of a statue of one of the key esoteric deities, the Six-Armed Guanyin.[29] The image is in disrepair, but when an old man appears and tells her it would be a meritorious deed to restore the image, she undertakes the project, and then wakes up. In accordance with a folk belief shared by many of the literati, dreams were seen in China, as they were in Europe for centuries, as prognosticators of future events. Sure enough, she stumbles upon what appears to the very image she had dreamed of, pays for its restoration by a skilled craftsman (another rare example of this branch of art being appreciated and praised by a literatus like Wen Tong, as in the previously mentioned text on Buddhist art in Sichuan), and eventually gives birth successfully.

Even more unusual is Wen's utterly unanticipated praise (in prose no. 1), for the *Sutra of the Eight Teachers (Bashi jing)* commented upon in this way by Robert Gimello: "The translator of this text [from Sanskrit into Chinese]—Zhiqian d. ca. 252)—is one of the earliest cohort of translators. [He was] a layman of Kushan ethnicity. . . This text is one of those [translated by him] accepted as genuine. . . even though there is no surviving Indic text that can be identified as corresponding to it."[30] (This last aspect is true of many Chinese and Tibetan Buddhist texts translated from Sanskrit or Pāli; that is, the Indian originals have been lost, probably because of the virtual extinction of Buddhism in its motherland at the hands of Muslim invaders in the eleventh century.)

The "Eight Teachers" turn out to be Buddhism's "Five Basic Precepts"—proscriptions against killing, stealing, sexual offenses, lying, and drinking intoxicants—with the addition of old age, sickness, and death. One "learns" from these how to live a wise life.

What is really characteristic of this text, however, is that Buddha, who is the speaker, lays out in horrifying detail the punishments in one of the various Hells recognized in Buddhism for the various offenses.

---

29 According to Robert Gimello (personal communication), "The male Guanyin was never really replaced by the female version (even though, at the popular level, he may seem to have been). Several other forms of Guanyin—all male (although often depicted as virtually sexless)—persisted." I am deeply indebted to Professor Gimello for his help with Buddhist issues.

The Fogg Museum at Harvard holds a banner from Dunhuang dated to 985 depicting a six-armed, eleven-headed Guanyin clearly displaying a moustache (see p. 215). Thus the image discussed by Wen may well have been male rather than female. For the most extensive study of Guanyin, see Chün-fang Yü, *Kuan-yin: the Chinese Transformation of Avalokiteśvara* (New York: Columbia University Press, 2000).

30 Personal communication.

For example, those who commit murder "upon death enter Hell, where they are roasted, drawn and quartered, and condemned to ten thousand evil measures in rotation. Should they plead for actual death, their plea will be ignored. Only when the sin is purged may they emerge."

5

There had existed, down through the centuries, what might almost be called a Fourth Teaching, in some respects pre-dating Confucianism (sixth century BC), Daoism (of contested date as an "organized" body of thought, but the basic components in place by the fourth century BC), and Buddhism (arrived in China in the first century, possibly earlier). It is so foundational in Chinese civilization that it goes nameless, and might best be called simply "folk religion." At the same time, once the recognized Three Teachings were established, folk religion absorbed elements of all three, in actual practice leading to various eclectic mixes. Conversely, religious, or alchemical Daoism in particular, came to be based upon elements that preceded it in folk religion, intermixed with specifically Daoist ideas from the *Zhuangzi* and the *Dao de jing* (*Classic of the Way and its Power*, from perhaps the third century BC with earlier layers).

The relationship of the literati scholar-officials to folk religion is difficult to grasp fully, precisely because the practices in question were never systematized. What is more, modern scholarship, with its secularizing tendency, and starting as early as the *philosophes* of the Enlightenment, especially Voltaire,[31] has strongly emphasized the "rationalist" nature of the literati, almost seeing them as forerunners of modern intellectuals. This view is not without merit, but does overlook the more complex situation that emerges from a close reading of literati writings across the board, very much including poetry. Wen Tong, as it happens, demonstrates in his poetry and in certain of his prose writings, including official

---

31   Voltaire does in fact protect the notion of a supreme Being in his account of Chinese thought, consistent with the Deism he advocated: that is, a deity essentially remote from daily life. Such an idea can indeed be extrapolated from the Confucian *Analects*, but by the same token, the Jesuit missionaries, starting in the sixteenth century, were able to discover in the Chinese classics references to a Lord on High which they interpreted as references to the supreme God of Abraham and Isaac, along with prefigurations of the Incarnation and other key events of the Christian worldview. For an excellent summation of these matters, see D.E. Mungello, *Curious Land: Jesuit Accommodation and the Origins of Sinology* (University of Hawaii Press, 1985).

documents submitted to the throne, an interesting contrast to the picture of the literati as complete secularists *avant la lettre.*

On the one hand, Wen does echo what often seems to be the *suspiciousness* of the literati towards practices of folk religion. A perfect example would be his poem (3):

An Ancient Shrine at Phoenix Mountain

The trees of this wood are twisted, broken,
    the hall is falling apart;
Clay deities are still present, scattered
    chaotically on the floor.
A crazy shaman leaps and stamps,
    old peasants bow their heads;
With scrawny chicken and weak wine
    they invite the gods to dine.
Forms weird, perverse,
    snakes and serpents wildly writhe,
Cries and caws cacophonous,
    owl spirits screech . . .
The Ox of Disaster, the Hound of Catastrophe
    make their appearance too:
With such displays, how will our world
    ever return to peace?

The poem describes a local shamanistic ceremony; the villagers are dressed in costumes, impersonating various figures from the extensive pantheon of Chinese folk religion (some of these found only in certain locales, as the religion shifts and changes, reflecting local beliefs). Wen Tong crafts a wonderful poem here, adopting the conventional theme of a visit to a decrepit or even totally abandoned Buddhist temple, with the poet feeling a poetic nostalgia for bygone glory—parallel to Wordsworth's feelings at Tintern Abbey; here, there is an interesting tension between the collapse of the temple structure and its icons and the lively if unsettling (to the poet) antics of the villagers in their frenzied performance of a religious ceremony. Instead of the aesthetically attractive remains of a sacred shrine, we have the mere detritus of a ruined building, echoed in the "twisted, broken" limbs of the trees themselves, and generally embodying the "chaotic," "crazy," "perverse" nature of the ceremony. The snakes and owls that are here impersonated or present (or both) are creatures of the night, and of ill omen. The whole scene is like something out of John Buchan's great novel of witchcraft in seventeenth-century Scotland, *Witch Wood* (1927), even to the underlying ambiguity as to the degree of spiritual actuality in the events. Wen Tong in his last line leaves no room for doubt, however, that he sees the scene as a display of *chaos*, as opposed to the peace for which he yearns; as in Buchan's novel, yes, this is evil.

And yet elsewhere, on the contrary, one gets the sense that Wen Tong subscribed to some of the underlying beliefs of folk cults, rather than scouting them without question as incredible. (Of course, there are really two questions here: (1) Is it good, or bad? (2) Is it ontologically *true*? That is, do such deities exist or not? If so, are they capable of a response to human petitions?) To return to the Buddhist *Sutra of the Eight Teachers*, with its account of various punishments in Hell, we would certainly expect the literati of Voltaire's imagination, for example, to reject the whole concept out of hand. In fact, Wen Tong's cousin and admirer, Su Shi, upon viewing a set of paintings of Hell by the great Tang master, Wu Daozi (whose works are no longer available, despite several claimants to the honor of being authentic products of his hand) describes how when these were first displayed in public, people were so terrified that for two months they stopped slaughtering animals (one of the sins for which one would be punished in Hell). But Su's *gātha* (a Sanskrit term for a sacred hymn) on the subject[32] leads to an assertion of skepticism:

Gātha on Images of Hell

I have heard when Master Wu Daozi
First painted images of the Ghost City,
Folks in the capital, afraid of evil *karma*,
For two months stopped animal slaughter.
But these paintings show no true phenomena:
Brush and ink assembled things all false.
It's like trying to get full by *speaking* of food:
Why, then, did they tremble and perspire?
Thus we realize the *dharma realm* by nature
Is all of it created by the mind.

---

32 Su Shi, *Dongpo qi ji* (*Seven Collections of Dongpo's Writings*) edition of the *Sibu beiyao*), Vol. 2, 40/6b.

Once one realizes this truth,
Hell naturally crumbles away.

Su here clearly states that the images are all mental, so there's no need to fear. Upon realizing this, Hell will be destroyed naturally; that is, one will grasp that the whole thing is an illusion. We find similar ideas in such a text as the Tibetan *Book of the Dead (Bardo Thodol)*[33] with regard to the horrific deities that play such an important role in Tibetan Buddhism or Lamaism, as well as in esoteric Buddhism in general; that is to say, they are taken to represent states of mind, rather than being, again, ontologically real deities. (It is unclear whether Su is putting forth a version of this doctrine, or simply expressing broad skepticism.) Of course, in Buddhism, the very idea of "reality" is moot; all is illusion. But one wonders about the extent to which this concept took hold among the masses of devout believers. What is more, in such a text as the *Sutra of Eight Teachers*, Buddha himself certainly appears to be enlisted on the side of those who take Hell very seriously indeed.

How, then, did Wen react to his reading of the text? In his own words:

At first, I thought that these (descriptions of Hell) were simply incredible; but frequently they would be brought forth to admonish and influence worldly manners, and this produced results. My friend, Lü Jinshu, Editor of the Imperial Library, has described *The Sutra of the Eight Teachers*, narrating the events that occurred to the Chen clan in full detail, and in confidence has told me of his own personal experiences with regard to these matters. Jinshu is by nature stolidly upright and rational. His statements are never fallacious. I subsequently acquired a copy of this text, and took it home with me to Sichuan, where I hoped to have it printed, so as to promulgate it. My idea was that should there be in the world anyone acting perversely and violently, devoted to a life of illicit action, although such a man might congratulate himself on avoiding official punishments of the Dynasty, and thus living until he dies avoiding a catastrophe from Heaven and keeping his hide whole, this text would indeed make him aware that within the Abysm of Hades the ordinances are bitterly cruel, and there is no way he can hope to be whitewashed, and thus get to escape!

---

33   See the translation by W. Y. Evans-Wentz, published in 1927.

> And so by means of fear, perhaps it will be possible to change his heart and reform his actions, undergoing personal contrition and confession. For this *sutra*, should today's men convert through it, will establish great examples of brilliant results . . .

One might think that Wen's brief is for something like the idea promulgated by the *philosophes* that without believing oneself, one should support the role of religion in society, because it is salutary for the masses to believe in these things. But Wen clearly goes beyond that, in citing the testimony of Lü Xiaqing (Jinshu, 1015/18–1070),[34] who was indeed one of the editors of the *New History of the Tang Dynasty*, coordinated by Ouyang Xiu. (He, like Ouyang, gathered epigraphic inscriptions and published them in a book. Ouyang Xiu has a poem seeing him off.) We are unfortunately given no details here of his "personal experiences," nor of the incidents that the "Chen clan" experienced, but the assurance that Lü was "upright and rational" is clearly calculated to alleviate any suspicion that he was "superstitious." The implication is that there actually is *something to it*.

With regard to Daoism in particular, it has long been recognized that there appear to be two major streams. As Herlee Creel put it,[35] "Philosophical Daoism" involves the great texts, the *Dao de jing*, the *Zhuangzi*, and the *Liezi*. These seem to date from the fourth century BC *(Zhuangzi*, parts of *Liezi)* and the third century BC *(Dao de jing)*, but these dates must be considered tentative, as there may be later additions to the first two, and the third may include earlier passages. When Wen Tong describes his "conversion" from Daoism to Buddhism, he seems to have in mind this type. But even after his serious involvement with Buddhism through the influence of Minxing and other monks he befriended, his interest in the second type of Daoism, which Creel called "Hsien Taoism" (Xian Daoism)—the quest for longevity, even immortality, by becoming an Immortal (*xian* 仙), and transcendence of the earthly plane through concrete practices such as breathing exercises, the imbibing of various herbs, properly prepared, and the alchemical concoction of an elixir of immortality—his interest in actually pursuing some of these techniques

---

34   For more on Lü, see Li E, *Songshi jishi*, Vol. 1, p. 397. Li presents one poem by him. See also Chang Bide *et al*, *Songren zhuanji ziliao suoyin*, Vol. 2, pp. 1215–1216.

35   Herlee Creel, *What is Taoism? and Other Studies in Chinese Cultural History* (University of Chicago Press, 1970), Ch. 1.

appears to have remained strong. Poems 139 and 148, for example, detail his cultivation of Daoist herbal preparations; in poem 141 he actually requests some elixir from a man reputed to have successfully concocted it. That Wen broke ranks with the "elite," "philosophical" type and continued to be interested in the *xian* type appears to be unique, the opposite of what one expect from a member of the Chinese scholar-official class.

Where Wen Tong seems to be most engaged with what might be called a "folk belief" is in his relatively numerous poems and official "texts" (called *wen* 文, here a technical term for a particular *genre* of official memorial or report to the throne[36]) dealing with prayers for rain. As magistrate of various locales during his official career, Wen was obligated to function as a kind of priest on behalf of his people during times of drought, or excessive rainfall, both of which spelled catastrophe for the crops and thus the annual harvest. What might be called the priestly role of the local magistrate has gone largely unnoticed, partially because of the ingrained idea that these were merely secular figures. But at times of drought, for example, not only were the magistrates assumed to take this role, they might be explicitly ordered to do so, as Wen informs us in the following text[37] (prose no. 11):

Receiving an Imperial Command to Pray for Rain
while Sacrificing to Mount Zhongliang

On such-and-such a day of such-and-such a year, because of a prolonged absence of rainfall and subsequent drought, the court commanded that the local magistrates each within his region *personally* offer sincere prayers. I respectfully undertook an excursion to Mount Zhongliang, where I offered sacrifice to such-and-such a deity [the deity of the mountain], stating the following:

"From the imperial domains unto all the provinces of the Dynasty, and from last winter unto the present autumn, the evil Drought Demon has freely unleashed his destructive harm. For the common folk, this has meant a lack of timely rainfall, leading to the

---

36   Ch. 36 of the *Wen xuan* (*Selected Anthology of Literature*), 530 AD, contains a number of texts designated *wen*.

37   For a study of such writings, see a recent MA thesis by Xiao Yuxia, *Songdai qiyuwen yanjiu* ("A Study on Song Dynasty Texts on Praying for Rain"), from Northwest Normal University in China (2013).

destruction of all crops, and the failure of the great fields, and to extreme difficulty for the people in finding food, and massive numbers of them taking to the roads, without any other recourse . . ."

The emperor, we are next told, began by *submitting himself to austerities,* such as fasting, in the hope of moving the gods to send rain. This is a reminder to us that if the local magistrates sometimes functioned as priests, the emperor was the archpriest, and held himself responsible to "the gods" and ultimately to Heaven in his obligation to help the people. But in this case, Wen writes, there was no response. And so the emperor "issued a special proclamation, commanding local officials to visit those places within their jurisdictions that had deities listed in the official records, and there *personally* to offer the good things to eat in sacrifice to gods [in charge of rainfall] . . ." (The gods in question would have to be "listed in the official records" at court; otherwise they would be considered heterodox.)

Wen, being one of the officials in question, performed several such ceremonies, recording them in his *wen* (see prose nos. 14–19). It is apparent from these that several deities are involved, including of course the "dragon gods" understood to be in control of rainfall. These are local gods, enshrined in the specific area involved. One of them, for example, is a female dragon god, who because of her great generosity in sending rain had a special shrine erected to her in Chengdu, and was further accorded the honorific title Ruisheng Furen (Lady of Sagacious Wisdom), the subject of prose number ii in the series 14–18:

Text on Sacrificing to the Lady of Sagacious Wisdom

It is the case that you, our Lady, once promised the Master of Methods that you would seek to protect this our region. Today, the *yang*-sun force is raging with drought, and the Many Crops are about to fail. Your Ladyship and your household are expert at sending thunder and rain: if you have not renounced your vow, and are prepared to save this, your people, may you command that this be done, and you will enjoy sacrifices by the people of this land! May you endure as long as Heaven and Earth! We will also present this matter to the Master of Methods, so that he need not feel ashamed.

The Master of Methods is another deity, understood here to be the *superior* in the spiritual hierarchy. Wen lets out a subtle hint of irritation with the Lady's unsatisfactory performance thus far ("if you have not renounced your vow—to protect this our region") but promises that if she changes, she can expect plentiful sacrifices. He here plays the role of priestly intercessor for his people.

Elsewhere, Wen goes further than the subtle hint in this text: he directly berates the various gods for their apparent indifference to the sufferings of the people. In his unusual, if not unique sequence of three poems "Invocations Querying the God, with Preface" (320–22), he openly wonders why the god (apparently a local dragon deity) has not come through for the people, and challenges him directly. The preface this time is precise in giving us the date and the location of the drought. We are told that "the people rushed *en masse* to the Quintessential Proclamation Pond to obtain divine water." That is, they visited a pond where the dragon god was believed to be hibernating, in the hope that the "divine water" of this pond, taken home to their local shrines, would move the gods to send rain. But even this did not work. And so he, the magistrate-poet, felt compelled to intercede on their behalf (whether he is addressing the dragon of the pond, or the local dragon, is unclear). We will give here the preface and the first poem only:

In the fifth month, summer, of the year *bingshen* [1056], there was a great drought in Nanbin. The local people rushed *en masse* to the Quintessential Proclamation Pond to obtain divine water. As soon as they got some, they returned to their local shrines, there to pray for rain. And yet after more than ten days, there was no response. The people became terrified. The grain-crops withered away completely, and with nothing to eat, the people faced death. And they wondered, why did the god not prove his efficacy immediately, as he did in the past? All mouths opened in wails and sighs, and hearing them, I wrote these "Invocations Querying the God," and had them performed as songs. There are three of them in all, as below.

Upon the occurrence of this year's drought,
We called on all the spirits, but they were silent.
Calluses like molted silkworms, foreheads streaming sweat,
The people passed to distant regions, Yea!
Those whose gods had blessed them with moisture.

Carrying pots and jars, taking what extra drops they could, Yea!
Bringing them home in protected carriages.
They hoped for officials to pray truly, sincerely, Yea!
For some slight compassion on the people's starvation;
Shamans sang, shamanesses danced, Yea!
　　Tongues flapping, wrists drooping down.
In the plains they cried out, in the fields called, Yea!
　　Old men running, crones rushing too.
They wrote out fresh vows of purity,
　　spread them through their homes, Yea!
Presenting them repeatedly every day, with ever greater urgency.
I would like to query the god, Yea!
Have you no pity? Just what is it you're doing?

The shamans and shamanesses here, unlike those in the poem about the shrine at Phoenix Mountain, appear to have the poet's sympathy. These are the attempts on the part of the folks themselves to move the god, who is seen as a legitimate, "orthodox" god, rather than the illegitimate ones appealed to at Phoenix Mountain. Thus the dichotomy seems to be more orthodox vs heterodox than true (ontologically) vs false. What is more, if we look at the total picture provided by all these texts, we see a situation in which *every level of society*, from the emperor personally down to the magistrates personally, and still further down to the farmers themselves with their own shamanistic rites in the fields, are cooperatively participating in a single great religious ceremony calculated to move the gods on behalf of everyone. Needless to say, this is a conception radically distinct from the modern, Marxoid view of traditional society as consisting of different classes in conflict (or contradiction) with each other; hierarchical, yes—but this is a hierarchical structure beneficial to every level, and ultimately all participants are subscribing to the same unifying worldview. The literati may perform their role with attitudes ranging from skeptical or even cynical compliance to considered acquiescence or even full-fledged belief—but they unquestionably accept the belief system.

As poems, the three "querying the god" achieve an almost prophetic gravitas, although the prophetic voice is here aimed not at the people, for falling away from the god, but rather *at* the god, who is failing the people! This is accomplished in part through the meter employed. The poems are, in fact, not *shi* at all, but rather poems of the *Chu ci* type (also *Ch'u tz'u,* "Songs of the State of Chu," sometimes "Songs of the South"), associated with the poet Qu Yuan (fourth century BC). The meters of the *Chu ci* are based on various combinations of characters with the recurrence of the exclamatory particle *xi* 兮, which may be rendered, "Ah!," "O!," or as here, "Yea!"

Su Shi, writing after Wen Tong's death in one of his many expressions of praise for Wen Tong, says, "My late friend Yuke had four supreme skills: *shi* poetry was number one; *Chu ci* poetry was number two; cursive calligraphy was number three; and painting was number four."[38]

This makes Wen Tong the only Chinese poet known to me to be praised for mastering the *Chu ci* genre. But in reading his poems of this type, the three just mentioned, as well as others such as "The Terrace of Transcendence" (poem 312), and comparing them with the classic poems of Qu Yuan, it becomes evident that Wen Tong has simplified the often dense and flowery diction of the older poems in favor of a crisper, more straightforward diction of his own. He has thus put his personal stamp on this ancient metrical form.

Closely related to the contentious relationship with the god or gods, unnamed, herein addressed, are Wen's thoughts on a painting that depicts the *capture* of an unforthcoming dragon king, from poem xiv in the series 292–311:

> Why, oh why has that dragon
>   been exiled by Heaven above?
> Because he wouldn't follow Heaven's command
>   to bring fructifying rain.
> Thus Heaven commissioned the Thunder Duke
>   to seek him everywhere;
> But where had the dragon hidden himself?
>   Now, suddenly, he's caught! . . .

Clearly, even the dragon kings, powerful as they are, must answer to a higher power, Heaven. And Heaven is perfectly prepared to commission its operatives, such as the Thunder Duke, to do its dirty work. Of course, such a poem is playful and fanciful in tone, and is hardly intended as a *credo* of actual belief. But in his writings about the real world and his duties within it as a magistrate, as we have seen, a real relationship with the dragon kings and other deities seems to be conveyed.

---

38   Cited in *Anthology*, p. 194.

Thus we have in Wen Tong a man who was at once a "typical" literatus of his time, and yet an individual who made his own carefully thought out choices in life, as well as in literature and art. As an official, he demonstrated genuine concern about the people. In painting he single-handedly elevated bamboo to one of the major themes in the history of Chinese art, a position it would never lose. And in his writings he made innovative use of the ancient *Chu ci* meter, "modernizing" the diction of such poems, while also participating in the general move towards realism in Song dynasty *shi* poetry—in his depiction of the lives of different segments of Chinese society in his day, and in his expression of his own feelings. He was a man who searched for truth in all of the Three Teachings, and who gave an unmistakable personal touch to the often formulaic official writings he was obligated to submit, especially the "texts" on praying for rain and other related matters. A "renaissance man"? A "man in full"? Certainly more—*even* more—than we have realized he was.

Bibliographical Note

The original collection of Wen Tong's writings was edited in 1195, by Wen Tong's fellow Sichuan native Jia Chengzhi. This text has long since disappeared, but apparently formed the basis for the two oldest extant editions, both from the Ming dynasty Wanli period (1573–1619) and both of which follow the chronological organization established by Jia Chengzhi:

1. An edition titled *Chen Meigong xiansheng dingzheng Danyuan ji* (陳眉公先生訂正丹淵集, *The Collection from the Abyss of the Elixir as edited and corrected by Chen Meigong*), with preface dated 1610. Chen Meigong is the famed literatus, Chen Jiru 陳繼 (1558–1639). This edition is included in the *Siku quanshu*, as well as in both *Sibu congkan* and *Sibu beiyao*, and is available on-line at: www.kanripo.org
2. An edition titled *Xinke Shishi Xiansheng Danyuanji* (新刻石室先生丹淵集, *The Newly [Re]printed Collection from the Abyss of the Elixir by Master Stone House*), with preface dated 1612. This edition was printed by Pu Yiyi 蒲以懌, a local Sichuan official. A facsimile has been published in *Song ji zhenben congkan* (宋集珍本叢刊, *Collectanea of Rare Editions of Song Dynasty Literary Collections*), compiled and published by the Sichuan Daxue Guji Yanjiusuo (四川大學古籍研究所, Rare Antique Book Research Institute of Sichuan University), 2004, Vol. 9. This is the edition used for the present volume, and referred to as *DYJ*.

Although there are no modern editions, an anthology of poems with extensive annotations, *Wen Tong shi xuan* (文同詩選, *An Anthology of Selected Poems by Wen Tong*), compiled by He Zengluan 何增鸞 and Liu Taiyan 劉泰焰, was published by Sichuan wenyi chubanshe, Chengdu, in 1985.

The poems of Wen Tong translated here appear in roughly chronological order; both *Anthology* and *DYJ* use chronological order, as did the original edition of 1195, although the appropriate period in Wen Tong's life for some poems is a matter of speculation.

For reference and discussion, poems are consecutively numbered prior to their titles. Numbers following the poems refer to their page number in the *Anthology*, if they are included in that work, while all others are cited from the Wanli-period edition of Wen Tong's writings, indicated by *DYJ*.

A few samples of original texts are provided immediately before the relevant translations. These are to give readers of literary Chinese readily available examples of Wen's diction and style, given the relative difficulty of tracking down even the modern anthology cited.

Opposite: Detail from *Bamboo in Wind,* Xia Chang (1388–1740). Hanging scroll, ink on paper, full image 80 1/16 x 23 1/2 in (203.4 x 59.7 cm), ca. 1460. The Metropolitan Museum of Art.

THE POETRY
OF WEN TONG

1   *Mountain Moon Beneath Newly Cleared Skies*

Tall pines leak through pale moonlight;
Falling shadows seem to paint the ground.
Pacing, I love the scene shed below;
For long I cannot bring myself to sleep.
Scared by the wind, pond-lotus roll back leaves;
Spoiled by rain, mountain fruits fall.
Who accompanies me in my bitter chanting?
Filling the woods, chirp the weaving-crickets.   21

2   *In East Valley, following the little stream,*
among the thick copses is a round pool.
Loving it, I sit there long, and write what I see.

A wild creek flows into an ancient tarn,
Stone banks contain the whirling abyss.
No flying dust can ever enter here;
Bamboos and trees surround the pure current.
Peaceful I go, to have supreme enjoyment,
Lingering deep, escaping vulgar *karma*.
Cold beams shine clean my troubled breast;
The whole scene quiet, mind reaching a perfect round.
On a withered bamboo branch crouches a blue-green kingfisher,
Declining his neck to peer for sunken freshness.
Facing him, I do not dare to move:
I watch him—we are both immersed in Zen.   4

3   鳳山古祠

林木摧折堂廡傾；其中壤像猶縱橫
狂巫騰踏野老拜；瘦雞薄酒邀神明
形容詭怪蛇虺亂；聲音醜惡鴟梟鳴
災牛禍犬亦可作；世有此事何由平

3   *An Ancient Shrine at Phoenix Mountain*[39]

The trees of this wood are twisted, broken,
    the hall is falling apart;
Clay deities are still present, scattered
    chaotically on the floor.
A crazy shaman leaps and stamps,
    old peasants bow their heads;
With scrawny chicken and weak wine,
    they invite the gods to dine.
Forms weird, perverse,
    snakes and serpents wildly writhe,
Cries and caws cacophonous,
    owl spirits screech . . .
The Ox of Disaster, the Hound of Catastrophe
    make their appearance too:
With such displays, how will our world
    ever return to peace?   *DYJ* 4/6a

---

39   This poem describes a local shamanistic ceremony; the villagers are dressed in cos-
tumes, impersonating various figures from the extensive pantheon of Chinese folk religion.

4   *Arriving Late in the Day at a Farm Village*

These high plains have rock-hard earth—
    the stony way so narrow!
This hedge-lined alley shows, is lost
    in lingering, darkening day.
Old skirt fluttering in the wind—
    off gathering mulberry leaves;
White jacket wrinkled with moisture, back
    from planting seedlings of rice.
Tall cattails follow the winding stream,
    scattered oxen lie around;
Piles of wheat fill threshing floors,
    chickens fly wildly about.
The stream out front, the valley behind—
    dark evening vapors rise;
Children come out from each house now
    to shut the bramble gates.   7

5   *After Early Clearing, an Excursion to Repaying
     Benevolence Mountain Temple*

Mountain rocks jut craggily,
    the stone-cut road is faint;
Brushing pines, penetrating bamboo,
    dew now dampens my robe.
The mists open: on distant water—
    a pair of gulls descend;
The sun shines on the towering forest,
    a lone pheasant takes off.
The Hordeum-wheat harvest not yet in,
    they're late in tending the garden;
The little silkworms still "asleep,"
    they cut few mulberry leaves.
Evening mists now have closed in,
    sheep and oxen come down
As I let my horse find his own way
    back home through moonlit woods.   8–9

6   *Expressing Leisureliness*

Courtyard bamboo clustered in tall groves,
I move my bench closer to the fine breeze.
Closing the gate, beyond all work,
Leaning on the desk, forgetful of worldliness.
And what are they, affairs of the world?
In heart of hearts, we know them to be void.
Should a visitor come, may he not ask after me!
This feeling is vast and limitless.   9

7   *The Pure Sunbeam Pavilion of Magistrate Liu of Yongtai*

At tips of trees shines the risen sun;
Rolling up the blind, the morning sky is clear!
At studio window, reverie limitless;
Histories and documents touched by the pure breeze.
Dew has descended, soaking flowers heavily;
Windgusts come, floating bamboo lightly.
What need for me to disdain "five pecks of rice?"
Given all this, I decline Yuanming's[40] way.   10

---

40   Yuanming refers to Tao Yuanming (365–427), also known as Tao Qian, who famously gave up his official position, with its salary equivalent to five pecks of rice, to return home and go into a life of leisurely retirement. Wen Tong, describing official headquarters, notes that the place is already so serene there is no need for him to follow suit.

8   *The Thatched Study at East Valley*

> Rustic path turns to deep thickness;
> Serenity! Never marred by horse and carriage.
> Pine blossoms drop their golden powder;
> Moss leaves curl their blue-green growth.
> Insects and birds mingle spring noises;
> Mist and cloud turn evening colors dark.
> Where can vulgar dust ever enter?
> Always, the gate on the river is closed.   11

9   *Farmers' Huts*

> In gardens, morning air is fresh;
> Down hedge-lined alley, setting sunlight bright.
> At the rocky source the cold millstone is heard;
> On misty slopes evening plowing is seen.
> Pig's feet are offered, thank-offering to the gods;
> Tortoise plastrons[41] consulted for clear or cloudy days.
> If you would know the joy of a good harvest,
> The whole village rings with the sounds of dogs and chickens!
>   11–12

---

41   Tortoise plastrons and shoulder bones of cows and sheep were used in antiquity for the divination technique of scapulimancy. After questioning the deities or ancestors about weather, the wisdom of going to war, the condition of the crops, etc., heat would be applied to the object, which would form cracks. These were interpreted as answers from the spirits, and would be inscribed on the plastrons or bones as a record of the proceedings. Although these "oracle bones" display the earliest forms of Chinese characters known, they were discovered only well into the nineteenth century. Wen Tong would not have seen them, but he would have read in the classics allusions to the custom. Since it is unlikely that in his day actual scapulimancy was being practiced by the peasantry, Wen is conflating contemporary rural life with an Arcadian past.

10   *Evening Clearing at the Ink-Lord Hall,*
      Leaning on the Railing

Ink-Lord Hall—I view after-snow clearing;
Three miles of level forest
     spread out in frozen green.
Blue mist has gone
     to veil the distant shore;
White birds fly in
     to perch on towering trees.
The hoopoe comes to the garden,
     the silkworms already aged;
The yellow warbler passes the fields,
     where wheat is almost ready.
Seated here, waiting for the moon
     to break through east-ridge clouds,
I take hold of the blinds to raise them
     to an even higher hook.   14

11 *Returning Late from Gathering Herbs,*
Staying Overnight at the Mountain Hut
of a Country Man

> Shade hangs heavy from the eastern cliff,
>> shore peaks are very ancient;
> On both stream banks, waterfalls splash
>> where "goose-teat" stones[42] have formed.
> I have come from gathering herbs,
>> so late, I forgot to head home;
> I'm trying out staying at a bramble gate,
>> inquiring if there's chicken and rice.
> Spring winds fill the woods,
>> the lamplight burning cold;
> All night long, unable to sleep,
>> tormented by the mountain moon.
> At crack of dawn, stick in hand,
>> descending vernal vastness;
> Pine-needles in profusion everywhere,
>> washed by last night's rains.   14–15

---

42   "Goose-teat" stones are stalactites of a yellowish hue.

12   *Morning, Entering East Valley*

I've dangled hat-strings,[43] imitating the sovereign's officials,
Now I cast off my plow, return to my hometown.
Ten years, and only now have I come back—
The views all seem to have completely changed.
East Valley, a place that once I loved,
Suddenly before me—seems seen for the first time!
Misty clouds at morning attract my hiking stick,
For several miles I penetrate greenery.
Bright sunrise vapors shine on the stream-mouth,
On flowers and flora, dewdrops glisten like tears.
Tall pines twist up from high ridges,
Jutting upwards, thrusting their glorious trunks.
Casting shade, a mix of many trees,
Seeming to reach the empyrean above.
Flexible vines, as if linked to each other,
Occupying the turf, run helter-skelter about.
Long bamboos arise from their midst,
Ten thousand pointing upward like arrows.
I climb, look down, mourn for times gone by,
View and listen, pleased by these new joys.
I studied, once, in that decrepit thatched hovel,
The pathway bridge? Now broken, floated off . . .
Only the stream to the south of my house
Still spits out in foam from the same old rocky source,
Flowing, flowing, plunging down the dangerous valley,
Rolling, rolling, into a flying-silk fall.
Down by the side, I wash off my dusty lapels,
Gazing at reflections, and seeing there—myself!
Fame? Achievement? Really, where are they?
The road traveled has led to low station, solitude.
I raise my hand to wave at gibbons, cranes:
"I'm deeply shamed if I have startled you."   17

---

43   Officials wore squarish hats with strings that hung down and were tied beneath the
chin. The image is a synecdoche for official service.

13   *A Woman's Room in Spring*

Her pillow-wrap, suffused with springtime yearnings,
The window's silk lets through the morning light.
Spiders' webbing adds to the sorrow of parting,
The cuckoo's cry moves her with thoughts of faded fragrance.
Makeup box permeated with scattered powder,
She tries the old scent in the incense burner.
Here, in this woman's room, beside the lamp's flame,
There are only her dreams, reaching far away.   18–19

14   *The Pavilion that Pays Court to the Clouds*
       at Everjoy Mountain, Yanting County

The Long River here joins tall peaks,
Surrounded on all sides by crispest air.
From the middle flow, gazing up at cut-off cliffs,
Tips of trees show thousands of feet up.
A solitary pavilion appears up there,
Partially hidden, the size of someone's fist.
Master Li is Magistrate of this place,
And invites me to ascend the upper regions.
At this time, the sky-realm is clear,
And unclouded color washes clean the frosty morn.
Nature's Ten Thousand Images fill the four cardinal points,
And turning as one gazes, all can be taken in.
My soul now purified, I despise the dust below;
My desire here gratified, I joy in gibbons and birds.
We human beings love free openness,
But the world's work embitters us with annoyance.
Here I have gotten to climb and look,
And overflowing thoughts may fly like arrows shot.
The Magistrate tells me, "This pavilion was built by me,
And such fine scenes indeed must be quite few!
I'd like to have you pick a lovely name,
Whose glory will adorn the pines and mistletoe."
And so I named it, "Pays Court to the Clouds,"
And wrote these words, big, on a plaque above the mist.   20–21

15   *Stopping Late Along the River*[44]

We slowly make our way down to the riverbank;
Frosty winds invading our robes.
Fluttering, fluttering, geese land on the islet;
From far, so far, blackbirds regain the old wood.
The valley ahead is already thick with vapor;
Distant peaks still hold the setting sun.
In our lone boat, where should we go now?
Cutting the waves, we leave as if flying high.   22

16   *Flowering Plum*

Cold plum, reblooming on old branch,
Setting off bamboo, and hanging over pond,
Place where flowers, bedewed, now open,
Time when fragrance, sensed, flits quickly by.
Competitive, you invade late winter snow;
Exhausted, still enter springtime poems.
You gift me with your cold-season colors:
I love your look, just like frozen jade.   23

---

44   This is one of the poems praised by Ming poet Yang Shen (1488–1559) as on a level
with the greatest of the Tang masters. See Introduction (pp. 8–9) and *Anthology* (p. 35).

17   *Living in Poverty*

On rope bed, huddled in tattered blanket,
I get up early, hair not yet combed.
At southern window, I open a handscroll,
Going to sunlight to read on this cold day.
Before my gate, no carriages or horses;
At sunset, I'll hang a bit of mat to be the door.
On short garden walls, vines are hanging,
And hidden birds are pecking at the red fruit.
Troops of snails, so awful! form after rain;
They creep around, inscribing seal writing on empty walls.
When a man lives in poverty like this,
The universe seems too narrow for him to lift his head.
Fluttering about, a dove that can't fly over a tree;
Twisting and turning, a louse hidden in the threads of his pants:
Wife and kids all laugh at me,
Withered and worn, sticking to my brush and books.   23–24

18   *Living Back Home for a Period of Mourning*[45]

Mourning Period, back in mountain woods,
Insects and birds my daily companions.
My body suddenly has crumbled away,
Bones and flesh accustomed to suffering.
Vegetable platters? Ashamed if guests stop by;
Lying in sickbed—hate it when people talk.
The place so remote, who comes and goes outside?
The door of leisure sealed by heavy rains.   27

---

45   A son was expected to return to his parents' home to reside for a three-year period of mourning (sometimes curtailed to two years and three months), wearing rough clothing, eating a vegetarian diet, and generally submitting himself to various forms of ascetic practice. Upon his father's death, Wen Tong returned for a period during the years 1061–1063; for his mother's, 1067–1069. This poem was probably written during the second of these.

19   *Fifty Years Old*[46]

In my life, I never set my mind
    on pursuing lazy leisure,
But, in a flash, my years
    now measure fifty autumns.
Devotion to officialdom and literature?
    Quite shallow!
Alas! I've been exactly like that libertine,
    Li Mengzhou.   28

20   *Again Visiting the Mountain Temple*
    where I Studied of Old

The place where I once studied years ago,
Old temple huddling among the clustered peaks;
Unchanged, the colors of the winter of the year,
Still lovable, the pine trees at the gate.
The monks still here, but really aged now,
And much more relaxed in treating their visitor.
Again, I descend from among the white clouds,
While up in the bell-tower, they ring for evensong.   29

---

46   By Western count, Wen was 49 years old. Li Mengzhou, or Li Xiaozhen, an official of the early Sui dynasty (sixth century), while Magistrate of Mengzhou County would devote each day off to parties with music and wine, drinking all day long.

21, 22   *Autumn Inspirations, Two Poems*

i

Dawn winds blow through once-flourishing woods;
Evening dew settles on fragrant furrows.
Autumn's face changes, gaunt and sad,
As daylight once again gets ever shorter.
Soughing sighing, the year moves towards its close;
On and on, the season's signs transform.
I sigh out loud, leaning against a pillar:
All of this brings anguish to my heart.

ii

Hundreds of kinds of insects, moved by the *yin* of autumn,
As night comes on, their music still more shrill.
I ask them, "Why are you so bitter,
Crying 'til dusk without a break?"
Filling the courtyard, never stopping,
Swarming hordes hiding in ten thousand holes!
It may be Heaven has made them thus,
Helping to see off this season of withering.   33

23   *Visiting a Friend's Riverside Home*[47]

Hedge-lined alley leading down to cattails;
Gate of leisure closed—such is his pleasure.
Water creatures—"Shore-stick" clams among them;
Forest birds—a "Snatch-jug" pelican flies!
White waves sway my autumn skiff;
Blue mist covers the evening kitchen.
The host boasts of the country diet:
He boils fresh-grown vegetables for me.   34–35

---

47   Poems 23 and 24 are two of the poems praised by Yang Shen, see p. 8.

24   *The Pleasures of Leisure*

> Daytime nap, suddenly, past noon!
> Fine breezes blow over my bamboo cot.
> River clouds give rise to evening mist;
> Mountain rains send a subtle cooling.
> Bamboo-powder touches my robe, all moist;
> Orchid-scent perfumes my sleeping mat.
> Back home, at leisure, full of pleasure:
> Many thanks, Ink-Lord Hall!   36

25   *Living in a Village*[48]

> Sun-thrown shadows fill the pine-view window;
> Clouds part, the rain first tapers off.
> Woods under clear skies—pears and dates are ripening:
> On the street this morning, all the kids are glad!
> Oxen, sheep are way down by the creek-side;
> Ducks and geese are on the chilly pond.
> The farmers have just vinted their fresh wine,
> And send out jarsful, gifts for the next village.   37

---

48   The two first translations of poems by Wen Tong ever published are "Morning" and "Evening" in Launcelot Cranmer-Byng, *A Feast of Lanterns* (London: John Murray, 1916), p. 79. These turn out to be the first ("Morning") and second ("Evening") halves of this poem, each expanded from four to seven lines in the English, fleshed out with new material added by the translator. Cranmer-Byng's translations are rhymed, but not in accordance with the classical rhyme-scheme of the original.

26–35   *Ten Poems on Mr. Pu's Villa*[49]

i *Square Lake*

Wind blows reeds and cattails crazily crisscross;
Mist cut off, ducks are now seen flying.
Sunset—a single flute sounds out;
In a tiny boat, a fisherman, returning from fishing.

ii *The Pavilion Suffused with Blue-green*

At verandah window, morning breezes, fresh;
On mat and pillow, clear-sky radiance, cold.
A man relaxing in the pavilion—
His whole body trembles, reflected in the water.

iii *The Hall of White Lotus*

Pressing against the blinds, displaying pure colors,
Entering the chamber, offering fresh fragrance.
What best accompanies summer-heat drinking?
Facing these, we set flying our jade cups!

iv *Magnolia Stream*

Morning haze moistens the flowers' colors;
Clear-sky brilliance shoots light off the water.
Who has unveiled new tie-dye patterns?
They don't even worry about the autumn frost.

v *The Fish Pond*

Accumulated waters, deep, so deep . . .
The source constantly bubbling and gurgling;
There, on the shore, a kingfisher with blue-green robe:
Right before me, he takes his sudden dips.

---

49 The text of this poem series is largely effaced in the *DYJ*; see the text from the Chen Meigong edition, as reproduced in the *Siku quanshu*, 3/13a–14b. The *Anthology*, pp. 37–39, presents six of the ten poems.

vi *The Lotus Pond*

Purple canopies, softly glued to the water;
Jade stalks, long, stabbing the sands.
Avoiding the wind, reds showing, then hiding;
Startled by rain, greens crisscrossing each other.

vii *Bright Moon-Toad Bridge*

In river radiance trembles the jade disc;
Cloud-shadows open, reveal the golden platter.
Who is this, companion to my inspiration,
On the patterned bridge, leaning on the zigzag railing?

viii *Rice Paddies*

Water released flows round the crosswise canals;
Intersecting dyke-paths form chessboard squares.
The autumn wind announces fall ripening;
The acres all filled with breeze-blown plants.

ix *The Hall for Paying Court to Immortals*

The tall terrace links to the Realm of Voidness,
Flying equipages on display in the highest sky.
Lesser Omen[50] wearing Sacred Tiger token
Often comes here on crystal-clear nights.

x *The Thatched Hut*

Deep, deep, ensconced in Immortal Zheng Valley,
Tiny, tiny, this "Retreat of Jiao Guang."[51]
Should we inquire, "What is collected here?"
The bed is covered with books on reclusion.   *DYJ* 3/10b–11a

---

50   "Lesser Omen" is the name of a Daoist Immortal.
51   Jiao Guang was a recluse of the late Han who appears as a character in *Romance of the Three Kingdoms.*

36   *The Mountain Temple at Cangxi River*

Precisely noon: the seasonal heat intense;
So I moor the boat here, in Canxi River county.
Tiered cliffs embrace the forests,
There is a temple hidden in the greenery.
Leaving the boat behind, I climb the steep stone-step path,
Beneath thick shade, it twists and turns a lot.
Arriving on top at the home of golden Immortals;
Arrayed against the sky, rows of terraced halls.
Where long bamboo thrives hang waterfalls . . .
Sit there, feel the flaming heat change to cool.
An old monk understands how to discuss *sutras*:
How penetrating, insightful are his words!
He leads me up to the tallest tower,
And from that railing, I look down to the river below.
Quiet, remote, for over thirty miles
The landscape is everywhere a wondrous sight.
Who would claim that in the midst of travel,
What we get to see is always anticipated?
On islets down there, the white birds congregate;
From residences and villages bluish smoke scatters.
Delighting in all of this, at dusk I've forgotten to return
As sparse bell-tones arise beside the precipice.
Lingering, I finally reach the gateway below,
Still surprised to hear the boatman calling me.   39–40

37–46   *Ten Poems on the Eastern Garden at Langzhou*[52]

i *The Tower of the Embroidered Screen*

The thick wood all mottled, like embroidery;
The lush mountains jut up like a screen.
What is the best spot for climbing and viewing?
Where the railing lifts high into the depths of space.

ii *The Terrace of Fresh Winds*

At any time they will come and blow,
There are spots where you can look from even higher up.
When guests arise from their Pure Talk[53] conversations,
In great profusion fall hairs from their yak-tail whisks.

iii *The Pavilion with Views on all Four Sides*

The patterned screen once raised, no obstacles!
All precious copses now are in full leaf.
I want you, Sir, to appreciate them all around:
Don't just concentrate on a single angle.

iv *Willow Bridge*[54]

Pressing against the wind, showing off its evening look;
In falling rains, shrinking from spring cold.
Let me ask:
    What fragrant thoughts are you thinking of inscribing?
Who's that person, leaning with you against the patterned
    railing?

v *The Winding Pond*

Water glittering as if with pearl earrings,
Pond shaped like an arched jadestone chime;
Leaning over the ripples, just enjoying myself:
Fishes! Birds! Don't worry about me at all.

---

52   Two of these poems appear in *Anthology*.
53   The guests are engaging in "pure talk," discussing with wit and scholarship fine
points of philosophy, and holding emblems of didactic authority, yak-tail whisks, found
both in Daoist and Buddhist practice.
54   Bridges are where lovers may leave signs of their affections, poems, or today, fastened
locks.

vi *The Terrace of the Brilliant Moon*

The slight crescent rises from a corner of the sea;
Then the round dark disc reaches the heart of the sky.
Refined guests only are allowed up to this place:
Absolutely no hearts reflecting the world's vulgarity.

vii *The Triangular Pavilion*

They joined the timbers, and they formed acute angles,
Ran the railings, and these formed "teeth."
It was always from following the land's natural formation,
Not that they wished to make "points" and "slants."[55]

viii *The Flower Embankment*

Following the twists and turns, penetrating red blossoms,
Mottled and lovely, stepping on a rug of purple moss.
Who brought out this portable embroidered screen,[56]
And opened it expressly for the Inspector to view?

ix *The Herb Enclosure*

Jadelike bamboo shoots evenly sprouting toward the sun;
Golden bowls of blossoms at the season of flower-competition—
Naturally all of them are truly lovable:
May no painted blinds be hung to obscure the view!

x *The Intendant's Retreat*

You've already built a circular wall as an enclosure,
And planted here a moon-shape as your bed.
You come at times, and lean upon the desk,
Self and world transported to Fuxi's[57] imperial reign.

DYJ 5/11a–12a

---

55   The poet is eager to absolve the architects of doing things just for "effect." There
must be a natural connection to local *fengshui*, or geomantic patterns and lines of force.
56   See poem xxix of the series 197–226 for a related use of the "portable screen" image.
57   Fuxi, a major culture hero of China, reigned over a world of perfect peace in high
antiquity.

Studying in the Shade of Wutong Trees, Zhang Yin (1761–1829). Handscroll, ink and color on paper, 52¾ x 11⅝ in (134 x 29.7cm). Courtesy of Sydney L. Moss, Ltd., London.

47–48   *On a Summer Day, Leisurely Written on a Wall of the Ink-Lord Hall*[58]—*Two Poems*[59]

i

> My ancestors had a dilapidated hut,
> Here on the eastern bank of the River Pei.
> Now I, having left the governorship of Han
> Return to this place to rest myself awhile.
> The season is summer—fifth and sixth months,
> A red sun scorching in the distant sky.
> Mountains, streams—all desiccated now,
> Flora, trees, completely withered, parched.
> Having briefly removed my dusty lapels,
> I now have supreme scenes all to myself.

---

58   Wen Tong's Ink-Lord Hall is also the title of poem 50. That it was a much beloved retreat is shown by Wen's request that Su Shi write a "Record of the Ink-Lord Hall." See *Dongpo qiji* in *Sibu beiyao,* Vol. II, 31/4b-5a.

59   The two poems offer an excellent characterization of a typical period of rest in between official postings, with a relatively rare fidelity to details of the narrative sequence. In the Song, generally speaking, postings were for periods of three years, with breaks such as the one described here. Wen Tong feels like legendary hermit Shang Ziping: even he felt he had to fulfill his life obligations before entering true reclusion. The official positions Wen was assigned to were equivalent to "Magistrate," hence the escort of horsemen as he travels in his official capacity.

Towering woods embracing deep foothills,
Pure shade veiling stone-embroidery.
Layered cliffs yawning open right outside my door;
Shallow rapids rushing in front of my windows.
I invite guests to play my simple *qin*-zither,
Detain monks so they can pour themselves the cold spring water.
Bamboo mat and white-stone pillow,
A comfortable spot—but must be often moved.
Suddenly I'm riding on brisk winds,
Gazing afar where stand clouds and mist.
Country feelings reach the height of buoyant vastness,
Vulgar worries—not a bit of that *karma* left.
Energized brightly, soul naturally happy,
Old worldly concerns here can be renounced.
But then I remember when I was a lowly clerk,
My burdens so heavy, weighing down my shoulders!
Piled on my desk were documents and files:
Dealing with each and every one, I forgot to eat, to sleep!
Forced to wear cap and sash in summer's great heat,
Sweat from my forehead would pour down in torrents!
I lived in terror of being reprimanded:
How could I consult my own convenience
     at such a time as that?
But now I happen upon peace in leisure here,
I'm astonished, as if dreaming of a journey to the Immortals!

But soon I must don the governor's emblem again,
And once more take off to go to Yangchuan.
It isn't that it's not pleasant in these mountains,
But affairs tug at me beyond my control.
Recluse Shang Ziping, his vow not yet fulfilled,
How could he write his own "Homecoming Ode"?

ii

I've come back home to live here in the mountains,
And so I really am a "mountain-dwelling man."
Relieved indeed of cap and sash,
For months now they have not touched my body.
I let down my hair among slopes of layered cliffs,
Wash clean my feet on the banks of the clear stream.
Stone-lichens mottle my documents and files,
Spring winds descend upon my robe and headcloth.
Here, in my hometown, are many old acquaintances;
I've no aversion to visiting them often!
Mountain delicacies, country brew;
They treat me as if I were an honored dignitary!
As soon as an invitation comes, I rush over,
As I love how they love me so truly!
I'm afraid we may betray the dictates of etiquette,
But that just serves to show how intimate we are.
And just as I'm in the midst of this summer joy,
Suddenly we encounter the Season of Withering!
Again I feel shame at the thousand horsemen escorting me,
Once more into the dust of the western road.   43–45

49   *The Jade Lady*[60]

Of brilliant, shining dawn clouds, ah!
Embodying haze and mist,
So seductively lovely, ah!
So serenely radiant!
Like the arching of a dragon, ah!
Or the soaring of the phoenix.
Instantly appearing in scintillating light, ah!
Then suddenly, she returns to the darkness.
Residing in a mysterious palace, ah!
Hidden within a divine abyss,
She orders all her ladies, ah!
To take command of precious streams,
To bring blessings to the people, ah!
For thousands and millions of years!
—And then, to receive rich offerings,
To gather at Mt. Zhong.   *DYJ* 1/9b

50   *Ink-Lord Hall*

I love bamboo![61] I plant it and I paint it!
—As if surrounded by beams of a kingly palace!
Within the high hall, they lean against a remote cliff,
On whitewashed walls, crisscrossing their spreading branches.
Their mountain shadows shade autumn serenity;
Their moon colors purify nighttime's void.
This austere elegance—only I enjoy it:
Who else can love this retreat of mine?   *DYJ* 5/6a

---

60   The Jade Lady, a goddess appealed to elsewhere by Wen during a prayer for rain
in a time of drought, is understood to be in charge of rainfall and other meteorological
phenomena. See prose no. 14. See also Su Shi, *Dongpo qiji*, Vol. I, 2/3a for a poem on a
cave dedicated to her, and his description of sales of "divine water" by quacks.
61   Throughout, the poet may be describing painted bamboo, real bamboo, or a com-
bination of both. See also poems 47–48 on the delights of Ink-Lord Hall, also Su Shi,
Dongpo qiji, Vol. II, 31/4b-5a.

51   *Staying Overnight at the Temple of*
      Transcendent Fruits[62] *Mountain*

On overgrown path I slosh through marshy ground,
Up dangerous ridge, ascend treacherous slopes.
But loving this residence so pure, serene,
I never tire of coming frequently.
The mountain monks are delighted to see me,
In great confusion, they throw on their saffron robes.
They then escort me to a seat in the front verandah,
Mountain fruits—cinnabar, sapphire—laid out.
Done eating, we walk the rustic paths,
Beneath clear skies, treading the fresh, soft sedge.
Reaching a rock,
     I pillow my head on an ancient protrusion,
Or lean against a pine, clutching its longest branch.
Tonight, I will stay here, in this temple,
As the eastern mountains
     spit out the round moon's waves.
The night so long, I cannot fall asleep;
Birds and insects accompany my poetic chants.
And straight through to dawn, the leaves are falling,
Certainly no song for vulgar ears.
The cliffside gibbons and the streamside birds
Must laugh at me for coming here so often!   *DYJ* 5/6a–b

---

62 The "fruits" (*guo*) of the title may have the same double meaning in Chinese as in
English: fruit growing in the mountain (wild or planted by the monks), or the results or
outcomes of one's actions, one's *karma* (the Buddhist meaning).

52   *Master Hai of Fule Mountain*

What man, then, is this man of men?
He is a Zen master of Fule Mountain.
In Chengdu I once met him in the past;
At that time, already he sat on the Dharma mat.
Twenty years have passed now since that time;
Alas that we've been parted for so long.
But yesterday I visited him at Lotus Stream,
Abandoning my oar, and taking to my hiking stick.
Turning, turning, circumambulating on dangerous stone paths,
I ascended to knock at the gates of the Golden Immortals.
And there in the woods I recognized his solitary grandeur:
Zen eyes even bluer with old age!
He led me beneath the blue-green cliff,
Boiled tea, brushed off a mossy rock.

I asked him about the *gong'an* of "The Second Moon;"[63]
In a powerful exposition he cited ancient translations.
But there's no way I can become his follower,
And receive beneficial instruction over the long haul;
With the flip of the hand, back to the dusty marketplace,
Lowering my head in shame before this man for the ages.

DYJ 5/6b

---

63   "The Second Moon" refers to a Chan Buddhist *gong'an* (better known in the West as a *kōan,* from the Japanese Zen tradition) expressing the illusory nature of a doubled moon seen by some people under certain circumstances. There is, of course, no such thing, but in Buddhism, even the first moon is under suspicion of being a delusion.

53   *After the recent clearing, the shade of the trees*
      along the stream has a cleanly washed feeling—
      I have formed these rhymes while gazing at the scene.

After the rains, the stream's flow is brisk,
Clear-sky brilliance, tangible, as if floating;
The towering woods cast thick shade,
Dark, dark, bannered canopies clustered.
Wheat is ripe, mulberry fruits perfection;
In joyful confusion, yellow warblers sing.
Tsika tsika start the new cicadas,
Juu, juu coo the young dove-chicks.
With evening stick I seek out tranquil regions,
Loosened sash, now wandering all alone.
I look down at my reflection in the whirlpool,
Wash my feet at the brink of the spreading flow.
I wish to say: "Are you harboring the world's worries?
Pursue this purified realm, and let them go!"
I can trust for a fact that my dreams tonight
Will not be of the sorrows of the dusty domain.   *DYJ* 5/7a

54　讀楊山人詩

秋高群山空，眾籟吐天竅。
霜飆擊林野，岩壑起哀咷。
蕭蕭寒月下，合若萬鬼嘯。
疑是太古魂，嚠嚠此中吊。
山人住中巘，側耳得清峭。
譜之入文字，滿卷冷雪照。
其聲太淒楚，勁澀皆古調。
俗尚正淫靡，惑者自誇耀。
山人持之歸，無乃取眾誚。
會有知此音，相逢當一笑。

54　*Reading the Poems of Mountain Man Yang*[64]

Autumn sky so high, clustered mountains—no people;
The myriad sounds blow forth from heavenly hollows.
Frosty gusts strike the woods and wilds,
In cliffs and gullies rise cries as if of mourning.
Austere and solemn, the cold moon descends;
Here's harmony as of ten thousand ghosts in chorus howling.
Perhaps they're souls from High Antiquity,
Yuuu, yuuu—lamenting in this place!
The Mountain Man resides on the central escarpment:
Cocking his ear he hears it clear and stark.
Notating the sounds, he enters them in his writings,
So the whole scroll is filled as if with frigid, gleaming snow!
The sounds indeed are cutting, dolorous,
Harshly biting, all to ancient tunes.
Some are vulgar, lewd and dissipated;
Others boastful of brilliant accomplishments . . .

64　If the title personage of this unique poem could be identified, and if his works survived, we might find that he was a latter-day Li He (790–816), known as the "ghostly genius" for the almost gothic atmosphere of many of his most characteristic poems. See J. D. Frodsham, *The Poems of Li Ho* (Oxford: Clarendon Press, 1970, and multiple later reprints by various presses as *The Collected Poems of Li He*).

The Mountain Man collects them and returns,
Quite possibly to encounter ridicule.
But should he meet a real connoisseur,
Together they'll enjoy a moment's laugh.   *DYJ* 5/8a

55   *Abbot Yi's Bamboo Staff*

Abbot Yi's staff of wondrous bamboo
Never leaves his hand, even when he is seated.
Carefully polished, all shiny and smooth,
Its austere "bone" seems to writhe dragon-like.
Branches in groves are full of strange knots,
Marching pair by pair, arranged *en face*.
And routinely, solitary tips emerge,
Above, below, or divided left and right.
How, then, was this one, unique,
Produced by Heaven, without any mate at all?
And from whence did the Abbot obtain it?
This is unprecedented in the world!
Had it not been used by the Abbot,
It would have rotted away with all the other trees.
I hope the Abbot will not throw it away,
Will treasure it like divine longevity.   *DYJ* 5/8a–b

56   *During a Rainy Period, Delighted that a Guest Stops By*

Constant rains, no one I can visit,
Ten days, stuck here in the house.
But then a friend thinks of my retreat,
As lonely here as a withered tree . . .
In noble carriage, he comes to this remote alley,
Descends, and sets out to bring me consolation.
He's brought wine,
    to flush red the face of this drooping willow;
He's wrapped up food,
    to fill the stomach of this famished mulberry.
Sunset, he and his attendants leave,
And I return to reading the same old book.   *DYJ* 5/8b–9a

57   *The Eastern Window*

Clustered elms drop fragmented bits of silver;
Drooping willows brush the air with light silk threads.
Lovely paddies are darkened by red fog;
Winding embankments, swathed in blue-green mist.
The shade of the fine trees now joins together;
The new songs of the good birds join in harmony.
The eastern window is already full of light
As I still sleep, huddled in bed on my pillow.   *DYJ* 5/9a

58   *Heavy Rain*

Startled clouds ride the long wind,
Heavy rains soak the ninefold world.
One hundred rivers come rushing down,
    bringing landslides in their wake;
With an angry howl,
    a single roll of thunder crashes loud.
Everywhere, flora and trees are decimated,
Amidst distant rumbling, cliffs and valleys roar.
The man in the high tower, sleeping at midday,
Is woken up—but still lies there, leaning on his elbow. *DYJ* 5/9a

59   *Mr. Ren's*[65] *Bridge of the Chiming Jewels*

The pure stream washes the blue-green cliffs,
Rolling, rolling, cold music falling . . .
Mr. Zichuan, loving the stream's sounds,
Built a bridge to span the precipitous gulley.
When the mountain wind shakes the pine-hung moon,
He leans on the railing to hear the blended splash.
And so he's named it "Chiming Jewels":
A name never used before by any ancient man.   *DYJ* 5/9b

---

65   Mr. Ren and Mr. Zichuan of line 3 are presumably the same person, although he remains unidentified.

60   *Visiting a Homeowner along the River*

> The traveler's road takes him to river country,
> Where people's homes occupy what seems a painting.
> Green woods follow the distant shore,
> White waters fill the level bay.
> The fish so big, "foot-long" considered small;
> The gulls so light, they're weighed here by the gram.
> Whenever will I be able to take my leave,
> And come here to join this "Man Who's Hidden Away?"[66]
>
> DYJ 5/10a

61   *Evening Feelings in the Eastern Garden at Qiongzhou*

> A respite from official duties, now's the time
>   to wear headcloth askew!
> How could folks outside the gate
>   know this household of clerk-reclusion?
> Tussling ducks now form orderly flocks,
>   flipping floating-heart leaves;
> Young chicks, innumerable,
>   knock about pine-tree cones.
> I take my *qin*-zither to the flourishing fields,
>   and play "Flowing Waters;"
> Set up a mat on the fragrant isle
>   and chant "Sunset's Rosy Clouds."
> As dusk comes on, here are my parents!
>   And here are all my kids!
> We are all together in this place
>   to enjoy pleasure that knows no limit.   49

---

66   Han dynasty thinker Wang Fu (fl. 82–167) wrote the *Discourse on the Man Who's Hidden Away* (*Qianfu lun*). See the translation and study by Margaret J. Pearson, *Wang Fu and the Comments of a Recluse* (Tempe: Center for Asian Studies, Arizona State University, 1989).

62   *Passing Rain—Deflected Tones*[67]

The chariot of the *yin* force flies through the void,
    loaded with driving rains;
As the rain passes, woods and pond
    all seem newly transformed.
Tamarisk leaves float on the ripples—
    fish eat them by mistake.
Pine cones drop on rooftops—
    birds, scared, think, "crossbow pellets."
White clouds hang among the trees,
    stuck long before rising again;
Blue mists moor among plants,
    forever before they scatter away.
This Proud Clerk of the East Garden[68]
    loves the towering bamboo:
Book clutched tight, he leans into the wind,
    hair a total mess.   50

---

67   The title notes that the rhyme-words have deflected as opposed to "level" tones; in this case, they all belong to the deflected category, *han* 翰, in the modern fourth or "departing" tone. Some consider this to be a *ci* or "lyric-type" poem.
68   A nickname given to the great Daoist thinker Zhuangzi.

63   *Inscribed on the Blue Stream Tower of*
Professor Shu of Jinyuan

> The jutting tower flies through air
>   as it spreads its wings:
> And down below, its reflection trembles
>   on the wavelets' face.
> Light wavering on the painted walls,
>   in moonlight dark then pale;
> Sounds snaking along the zigzag railing
>   as wind comes and goes.
> Darkening colors on all four sides,
>   as mist veils everything;
> Clouds at dawn, thousands of feet up,
>   where snow-capped mountains surge.
> The master here rules wisely, and
>   the folks bring no lawsuits!
> Each evening he climbs up here,
>   a winecup in his hand.   51

64   *Drinking Alone on the Tower of the County Yamen*

> Toward end of day, no official duties,
> Feeling at peace, as if living in high antiquity,
> On the county tower, a bright moon shining,
> With a jug of wine I face the southern mountains.
> My thoughts go beyond fame and fortune,
> As my mind wanders everywhere between Heaven and Earth.
> My entire life, I've never been a drinker:
> In such a scene, I'll aim for a reddened face!   52

65   *Lingering Autumn Beyond the Suburbs*

Sighing soughing the scenery
    teases the force of the cold;
I've seen all the fields beyond the suburbs,
    in this evening light.
Last night, starry frost
    fell mingled with moonbeams;
Filling the woods, red leaves
    flew down, veiled by mist.
Already, I've lamented the northern islet
    where the lotus have started to wither;
And I've grieved at the eastern hedge,
    whose chrysanthemums are thinning out.
But let me not be saddened by the time of year,
    wounded by seasonal change:
Right here in front of me, a cup of wine!
    Again, I'll force myself to drink.[69]   52

66   *Outside the Suburbs*

The city? Weighed down by the dust;
In these high plains I can shake it from my robe.
Evening clouds against vast, pale blue;
Autumn trees, half deepening purple.
The river air mingles with light haze,
Mountain radiance illuminated by setting sunlight.
And since I want the best views I can find,
I'll go home over the rustic bridge.   53

---

69   The poet reminds us that he's "never been a drinker."

67 *The Night Serene, Alone I Climb the Little Tower;*
    Seeing Things of Interest, I Have Written Them Down

> Jutting tower, slanting across the sky,
>   hidden rustic gate;
> Deep in the night, I've come to climb,
>   and long forgotten return.
> On water's surface, scintillating beams
>   moving along with the mist;
> Clouds like newly growing feathers
>   flying while framing the moon.
> Across the river, a village in reeds—
>   I hear a far-off flute;
> Back to the bay, a pine-embankment,
>   faint lights flickering now.
> In such a place, I naturally feel
>   the joy of chanting poems,
> Oblivious of flowers of frost
>   covering me head to toe.   53–54

68 *Echoing Mountain Man He Jing's Poem on*
    Crab-Apple Blossoms

> Because I love this fragrant bloom,
>   shining their red on the ground,
> I've leaned on the railing the whole day long,
>   facing the perfumed clusters.
> But late at night, suddenly recalling
>   how fine was the highest branch,
> Again I come, winecup in hand,
>   lit by brilliant moonlight.   54

69   *Sent to be Inscribed on the Hermitage of*
      Mountain Man He Jing

In front of your entrance spreads the cold lake;
Above your garden wall stand the fine mountains.
You, Sir, have forgotten power and profit,
In noble reclusion, you've lodged yourself between.
The ducks and drakes must share your happiness;
The mist and clouds already partake of your leisure.
But when will I have a moment to spare
To bring some wine, and appear at your pine-tree gate?   55

70   *Writing Down Things Seen Late in Winter*

Leaning on my cane, I stand on the level bank;
The cold's power is fierce as morning comes.
Snow melts, the mountains' colors so old;
Winds whistle, the sound in the trees is loud.
In lingering sunlight, a thousand crows dance;
Near a solitary cloud, a single wild goose cries.
Quite naturally, I'm moved by all these things—
Unawares, again I scratch my head.[70]   55

---

70   Scratching the head can be a sign of worry or of thoughtfulness. Once again, the poet is moved to a philosophical frame of mind by the wonders of nature. The poem imperceptibly moves from morning to sunset, so he has spent the entire day in these observations.

71   *Residing at Peng Mountain County*

    The county office is completely silent;
    The garden and pavilion offer so many scenes:
    Stream light illuminates the single-plank bridge;
    Tree-shadows shade the tall lookout tower.
    Mountain birds suddenly descend in pairs,
    Pond fish now and then jump into the air;
    The host has little of the sovereign's business:
    With letters and wine he enjoys the passing days.   56

72   *Inscribed on Elephant-Ear Mountain Temple*

    Turning with valleys, winding round cliffs,
        the pathway finally arrives;
    Across the forest in the distance is seen
        a single gateway through.
    The streams and mountains all exist
        somewhere beyond sight and sound;
    The terraces and halls are hidden
        deep within the heart.
    The trellis-work screen of the Image Tower
        is illuminated by lake sunlight;
    The *sutra*-pillar's jeweled ornaments
        seem shaken by Heaven's wind.
    My burdened life—back I go
        carried by the little boat:
    How I'll treasure the noble monks'
        explanations of suffering, and the Void!   57

73   *Descending Gold Rooster Mountain*

Gorges tightly bundle layered mist;
Mountains divided by just a few feet of sky.
Cliff gibbons and river birds
Seem like flying Immortals whizzing by.   59

74   *Inscribed on the Wall of Crane-Cry Temple*

Evening air darker, darker,
    getting especially cold;
Setting sun beneath forest trees,
    I start my horseback return.
But suddenly, someone reports,
    "Snow on the mountains out back!"
Again I ascend to Upper Purity Shrine
    to catch the view from there.   60

75   *Traveling Early on the Road to Anren*

Riding a horse along the river
    before the sun is up,
Fine breezes without limit blow,
    billowing my light robe.
Cold-weather cicadas chant at the moon—
    starting one after the other;
Wild ducks, startled up from the sand,
    fly off in parallel rows.
Tall, tall, the wineshop banners
    rise above the shore;
Fluttering, fluttering, fishing skiffs
    return from the neighboring bay.
All these images appearing here
    are coming fresh to me:
True it is, poetic feelings
    cannot be betrayed.   61

76   *Bamboo Tower*

Twisting corridors embrace the bamboo tower;
Austerely profound, and void at the heart.
Painted balustrades—I lean on each bend of the railing;
Tall bamboo—I love their subtle sparseness.
Dust from outside never reaches here;
My robe is always perfectly clean.
Whenever I come here to enjoy myself,
Mysterious feeling fills *qin*-zither and books.   62

77   *In Search of Spring*

My horse gallops as if on rolling wheels,
Three miles and more, out in search of spring!
Warm and comforting, sunbeams so beautiful;
Fresh and lovely, cloud-colors are all new.
Towers and terraces jut up from flowery forests,
The roadways are all lined with pine, bamboo.
I'll go buy wine from that village up ahead,
Then, happily, be an intoxicated man.   63

78   *The Pavilion Facing the River*

Hidden pavilion, remote, cut off from the world,
Right in the middle of the wild copses.
Close to sunset, I come here:
Is there anyone to enjoy the leisure with me?
Rolling up the blind, revealing the great wild,
Facing the building, several mountains out front.
And now to bring out the wine,
Happily dance in moonlight, then go back home.   64

79   *Buddha's Head*

[*Poet's note*] The scenery here is especially fine.

> Off from work, I often come
> > to this spot for relaxation;
> Azure waves, greenish cliffs
> > know how to hold me here!
> Then as if floating, back I go
> > right into the city,
> I glance behind at streams and mountains,
> > and simply feel ashamed.   64

80   *Nighttime Study*

> I've already snagged my degree—
> > could easily give this up!
> But if you haven't reached the root,
> > how can you dare to halt?
> Letters—a bookshelf full of books,
> > lamplight—a single lamp;
> All I can think is in a former life
> > these things were my boon companions.   65

81   *Inscribed on Tushita Heaven Temple*

Documents and files drive me crazy!
    I love a moment's leisure!
And so I've come in search of this ancient temple,
    and climbed to the solitary ridge.
Cypresses hide the whole pathway,
    narrow passage through;
Clouds gather over a thousand peaks,
    spreading in all four directions.
My distant vision has already followed
    flying birds beyond;
My inch-size heart again begs the old monks
    for peaceful rest tonight.
And if they loan me the space of just
    a single meditation room,
Lying there, I'll watch the votive-lamp,
    the single flickering light.   68

82   *Young Li Paints a Crane*

Dignified, noble—Bluefield Mountain stock;
Mystic grandeur, here on the plain silk.
Whole body charged with ten-thousand mile yearning,
Eyes fixed on the ninefold Empyrean.
Razor-sharp, the quills of displayed feathers;
Statuesque, bone-structure in full view.
And from whom, sir, did you ever learn this art?
No, it must have been intuition divine!
You received it beyond imagined forms,
You show it where your splendid brush sets down.
Xue Ji? Huang Quan?—should these masters[71] return to life,
You'd contest with them who really is supreme!   85

---

71   Xue Ji and Huang Quan were two master painters known for "bird and flower" paintings.

83   *Echoing Zhongmeng's Poem, Sitting Up at Night*

Roosting birds now startled up
    by the cry of an isolated goose,
Alone you lean on your hermit's desk,
    free of dusty labors.
Wind whistles at the northern door—
    frost-power weighs heavily;
Clouds encumber the southern mountains—
    snow-feeling surges high.
A brief nap, time to learn
    the effectiveness of tea;
Great cold, you should enlist wine
    in the battle for supremacy.
Your inkstone already iced all over,
    old lampwick burning low,
Still you face the piles of books,
    huddled in padded winter coat.   86–87

84   *Temple for the Promulgation of the Teaching*

A rural path leans dangerously
    entering the valley on a slant;
Twisting ridges, winding peaks
    crisscross with each other.
A full year, yet I've never come here,
    just because of the river;
This day, alone, I stroll around,
    only to see the flowers.
Misty clouds turn both shores
    into serene landscapes;
The whole building opens on streams and rocks,
    truly a quiet life!
I regret that caps and emblems
    have kept me all entangled;
I entered straight into the cage,
    and grow old still inside.   87

85   *Echoing a Poem by Zhang of the State Farms Bureau,*
      "Late in Autumn, Leisurely Gazing from the Eastern
      Tower of Soul Peak"

A straight railing bisects the shady side
   of Purple Essence Mountain;
Leaning here long, autumn light
   illuminating my traveler's robe.
A swath of mountains lined by streams,
   cold colors stretching far;
Ten thousand households: lamps alit,
   deep into setting sun.
Jing River rapids: tide now down,
   flocks of ducks gathering;
Qin Mountain ridges: clouds so high,
   a lost goose sinks below.
These scenes so majestic surely call
   for a winecup in my hand,
But—what a shame! So hard for a heart
   this homesick to get drunk!   90

86   *Spring Courtyard*

Spring enclosure: dark, dark,
    blue-green mists hang low;
Spring courtyard: quiet, quiet,
    morning light veils all.
Among the flowers, butterflies
    flit off with yellow pollen;
Above the moss, swallows fly,
    beaks holding greenish mud.
Two stands of tall *wutong* trees
    have just joined their shade;
A swath of new blooming flora
    all grown to the same height.
One little bird already knows
    the feelings of this recluse;
He flies down to the balustrade,
    singing toward my hometown.   91

87   *Passing Long-Life County*

I urge my horse up the steep slope,
Evening whip trembling with traveler's sorrow.
Startled by mountains filling my vision,
Every few feet, thinking of turning back.
Red trees embrace a rustic tavern;
White clouds surround the county buildings.
I should think—from here, looking north and down,
That lowest place down there would be Binzhou . . .   91

88   *A Summer Day in the Hall of Blue-Green Ripples*

>Lake water, azure, lapping, lapping,
>Cold ripples wherever I gaze on all four sides.
>Turtles, fish swim through the huge vastness,
>Ducks and drakes descend from the great void.
>Brisk air outside the poet's window,
>Crisp brilliance out in the fishing boats.
>My whole being, happy at such a moment:
>Many thanks to the north porch breeze!   92

89   *Impromptu at East Valley*

>Office business? Happily, few files!
>And so I get to wander through East Valley.
>The old mountains of home look much like these,
>Fine scenes, where I always linger long.
>Broken, floating again, stream clouds arise;
>This way, that way, rural streams flow on.
>Not yet the time to "brush off my robe"
>But just for now, I console my homesick sorrow.   93

90   *Dog Days of Summer—Tenth Day of the
      Sixth Month, in Jade Peak Garden
      Escaping the Heat, Encountering Rain*

In South Garden escaping the worst of the dog days,
So suited to my mood, I forget going home.
Outside the wall, valley clouds arise;
In front of the eaves, mountain rains fly.
In an excess of feeling, I think of lighting a candle;[72]
Seated here so long, I want to add on clothes.
And most I love how below the eastern cliff
The sound of a waterfall leads out to blue-green slopes.   93

91   *The Ferry Crossing at Locust-Tree Villa*

Clouds and mist floating softly,
      trees in distant haze;
The whole bank of people's houses now
      tinted by setting sun.
I'd like to go up to the higher plains
      and gaze back at this view,
But—what a shame!—The scenery
      is just like my hometown.[73]   96

---

72 To "think of lighting a candle" is to consider staying on after nightfall. Even at this time, it might get chillier at night, hence the thought of "adding on clothes." This is another of the poems praised by Yang Shen.

73 The poet does not want to be saddened by the memory of his hometown, for which he is homesick.

92   *At Tingkou*

> Beneath forest trees, flitting, fluttering,
>   swallow shadows slant;
> Filling the stream, fallen red leaves
>   off-setting people's homes.
> Up on the cliff, a solitary temple—
>   a jutting tower visible:
> There's someone up there, come alone,
>   climbing through sunset cloud.   97

93   *Echoing Zhongmeng's Poem on the*
      Whirlpool of the Stone Dragon[74]

> Clustered ridges press on the banks of Jing River:
> Here have gathered many folks to live.
> Up above, a stone cavern exposed
> Viewed from far appears a yawning mouth.
> Beyond tree-tips, clambering up by rope,
> You enter and—the path becomes still more a struggle.
> Surrounding the empty space stand stone walls,
> A width accommodating perhaps one hundred men.
> There's a huge bell—but who has turned it over?
> A gigantic cauldron—once long ago split open.
> From layered cliffs a cold waterfall flies,
> On topmost escarpments, strange trees march.

---

74   Poem 103 also concerns the Whirlpool of the Stone Dragon. The identity of Zhong-meng is unknown; one possibility would be Li Yu (1020–1069) a Suzhou man known for his poetry. This is one of many texts by Wen Tong indicating his particular interest in the cult of dragons as rain deities. But he emphasizes what appears to be the undepend-ability, if not fickleness, of these deities. Sometimes they respond, frequently they do not. Thus in this poem, the familiar theme of visiting a deserted Buddhist temple is adapted to a concern, most unusual in Chinese poetry, with the desertion of a folk-religion shrine dedicated to the dragon god believed once to reside in a whirlpool of the Jing River below. Magistrates were indeed called upon to "pray for rain" in times of drought; but at the same time, the cults of the local dragon gods seem to have had real meaning for the local people. It is a general characteristic of Chinese folk religion that certain deities are seen as efficacious—and therefore become highly popular—during certain periods, after which they mysteriously withdraw their aid, and other deities must be sought out.

Wind-gusts from the darkness seem happy, then furious:
Wild fogs are sucked in, and then spit out again.
Clear-sky haze presses up against your robe:
You wish to rest, but cannot stay for long.

I have heard a plowman claim
That in the past, here lurked a slithering dragon:
In those days, it often saved the folks from drought;
There's a rock-cut record, still not yet effaced.
But in recent years, he fears,
    this spiritual efficacy has been withdrawn:
One hundred prayers result in not a single answer.
At this time, the people from the village
No longer climb here to offer libations of wine.   *DYJ* 6/1a

94   *On the Last Day of Autumn, Accompanying my Friends*
    to Climb the Tower of the White Buddha

The precarious fane, hidden on the highest peak,
Solitary verandah cutting across the azure void.
We climb for the view, enjoy autumn's end,
Laugh, relaxed, in pleasure at this release from public duty.
Out here in the country, scenes enter the realm of painting;
In our gathering, the joy is worth writing into poems.
The doubled city walls are already tightly locked;
Our returning horses still can't help but linger.   *DYJ* 6/3a

95   *Climbing the Walls of a Mountain City—*
      Writing Down the Experience

Moved by seasonal change during a journey,
As across the sky spreads frontier darkness:
Disorderly geese flock to the cold island in the distance;
Clustered sparrows gather, deep in the evening forests.
Frost lies heavy, Jing River rapids rush forth;
Mists hang high, dune trees sink in dusk.
The year without purpose naturally ages:
Dark indignation[75] fills our climb for the view.   *DYJ* 6/3a

96   *Setting Out Early on Feng Family Avenue*

Afraid of the heat, we start our official trip at dawn,
On the high plain setting forth upon our journey.
Far, so far, passing through immense expanses,
—While the long wind blows constantly upon us.
A few scattered stars, some starting to sink,
The Milky Way still hanging in the southwestern sky.
At the tips of trees begins to appear bright light,
Flying beams emitting reddish brilliance.
Scintillating, a wash of clear-sky dew,
All things in nature absorbing the flowery moisture.
Brisk air permeates our inner bodies,
Last night's sluggishness?—not one iota remains.
In a frigid stream we wash ourselves, its crystal sweetness
Cleaning away every vestige of vulgar worries.
But still we're concerned about the fiery wheel's anger,
How for ten thousand miles it will roast
        the cloud-covered highway.   *DSJ* 7/1b

---

75 Wen and his friends may be contemplating the fact that not far to the northwest lies the alien Xi-Xia (Tangut) dynasty which has made several demands upon the Chinese Song dynasty.

97   *On the Road to Xianyang, Written on the Occasion of Clearing Skies at Evening*

Accumulated vapors, with evening all scattered;
Southern Mountain illuminated by setting sunlight.
Autumnal scenes everywhere in Feng and Hao;[76]
Ancient sorrow goes back to Sui and Tang!
Flora and trees are all shedding now,
Wind-blown mists naturally vast and vague.
At the guest quarters, of course we must dismount,
And, wine in hand, console our feelings in this foreign land.

DYJ 7/3b

98   *Late in the year, Climbing the Northern Tower of the Cloister of Pure Plainness*

At the edge of the clouds, I visit an ancient temple,
At the tips of the trees, look out from the precarious tower.
The wind is powerful, subduing flora and trees;
The frost has withered all, pleasing birds of prey.
And since Heaven's season is desolate and stark,
Human feelings too are grievous and lonely.
I think back to how far my home mountains are,
And my heart goes down with the sun, sinking in the west.

DYJ 7/3b

---

76   Feng and Hao were the twin capitals of the Western Zhou dynasty. For Chinese travelers, each province represented what was virtually foreign territory.

99   *On the Dangerous Road to Tanquan*

> A stream yawns wide,
>> dividing all the peaks:
> Where can we now inquire
>> whether the road's run out?
> So high, so deep, emerging from a well,
>> then entering another well;
> So twisting, so straight, ascending a switchback,
>> then descending another switchback.
> Reaching rock bottom, all of a sudden overlooking
>> steep slopes further down;
> On utmost summits—suddenly they plunge,
>> and we seem to *fly* ahead.
> On my way to my new county position,
>> I've no choice but to pass this way—
> And right in the scorching middle of summer's worst dog days!
>> *DYJ* 7/4a

100   *On a Hot Summer's Night Awaiting the Moon in the Courtyard, and Not Returning until Late at Night*

> Finally, few daylight flies are left, but—
>> plenty of nighttime mosquitoes!
> I cast off my white silk shirt, but still
>> can't conquer the awful heat!
> Alone I go to the central courtyard,
>> awaiting the bright moon,
> My entire body, covered with pure dew,
>> now dripping with golden waves.[77]   *DYJ* 7/4b

---

77 The last line means that, already covered with beads of sweat, he is now bathed in moonlight, often compared to golden waves.

101   *On Mid-Summer day, all my friends gathered at*
       Jade Peak, but I was unable to attend on account
       of illness. I have written this poem and sent it to
       be presented to them.

Last year at Mid-Summer,
    we were all in the Southern Garden;
Together we listened to the pure sounds of the waterfall,
    and toasted with cups of green wine.
Today? All of you again
    are holding a noble gathering,
While I, alone, lament that all I can do
    is move my sickbed to the western veranda.   *DYJ* 7/4b

102   *On the Plain of Shallow Water*

Northwest of Chun'gu,[78]
    the land lies like fish-scales;
In this place in ancient times
    arose the dust of war.
And it is said that today,
    beneath the walls of irrigation ditches,
Broken spear-points and fragments of arrowheads
    belong to the men who plow the fields.   *DYJ* 7/5a

---

78   The Battle of Chun'gu of 765 engaged the Chinese against the Tibetans.

103   *The Whirlpool of the Stone Dragon*[79]

> The thrust of the precipices encircling the emptiness,
>> the hole in the cut-off cliff—
> All four seasons can always be seen
>> clustered clouds and mist.
> Bringing a downpour to save folks from drought—
>> whenever is that done today?
> All that survives is an epigraph
>> recording deeds of yesteryear.   *DYJ* 7/5b

[*Poet's note*] There is also a record by a certain Li Huai narrating in full detail the occasion of a successful prayer for rain here.

104   *Evening View from the Abbot's Quarters of Calm Residence Cloister*

> Winding round cliffs, circumambulating valleys,
>> I arrive at the Zen quarters,
> Then even further, the highest point,
>> the pavilion at the top.
> The wind compels wild-flying crows
>> to circle ancient trees;
> Rain forces a flock of herons
>> down to a cold landspit.
> The ditch-banks of the autumn fields
>> are laid out like chessboard squares;
> Peaks and ridges of evening mountains
>> resemble a folding screen.
> My poem is almost finished now,
>> as night reaches its end;
> In distant villages, lamps are lit,
>> each a flickering star.   *DYJ* 8/2b

---

79   Poem 93 also describes this place, explaining the tone of disappointment or frustration of the last two lines as well as the reference to a textual record of earlier successes in enlisting the aid of the dragon god against the drought.

105　*Auspicious Cloister*

Leaning dangerously, a single path gets through;
Dismounting, I turn into deep woods.
This realm lies beyond the dusty world,
So wonderful!— here, at the misty embankment.
Tall bamboo drip coldly with rain;
Ancient cypresses—serenely set chanting by the wind.
Sunset, and to trees outside the courtyard
Homing crows return from distant void.　　　　　*DYJ* 8/7a

106　*Reading History*

He failed to win at Yingyang,
　　and thus lost his chance at Qin:[80]
From this I know *success or failure*
　　depend entirely on the man!
Alas, with just a single throw
　　he lost the entire world,
And all it took was yellow gold,
　　forty thousand catties worth.　　　　　*DYJ* 8/9b

80　This is a comment on a key failure by Xiang Yu, first the putative ally and then the rival of Liu Bang in the effort to overthrow the Qin dynasty (221–206 BC) and to found a new dynasty. Xiang Yu was thwarted militarily at Yingyang, but also lost the allegiance of several of his commanders who, according to one tradition, were bribed by Liu Bang's agents with 40,000 catties of gold. The second line here is a rare, explicit acknowledgement of the great timeless question—whether the events of history are driven by Heaven (fate), or by decisions made by man—a tension that runs through Chinese historiography and indeed transcends the Chinese case. In modern times, "fate" may be substituted for by mysterious social and economic "forces" that appear to have a life of their own independent of human choice. An excellent modern description by a Western writer would be the opening chapter of the novel *August 1914* by Aleksandr Solzhenitsyn. Wen Tong, like Solzhenitsyn centuries later, leans toward personal choice as crucial in determining historic outcomes, seeing Xiang Yu's failure ultimately as his own fault, whereas Xiang Yu himself famously declares, in Sima Qian's (ca.135–86 BC) account of his struggle with Liu Bang, that: "This is a case of Heaven dooming me, not of any fault of mine in battle."

107   *The Wang Family Forest Pavilion at Hanzhou*

A short plank-bridge, a few spare hedges,
　　lead to the rustic gate;
Bamboo mist and pine-tree dew
　　fill my robe with purity.
Rushing rapids—torrent so wild!—
　　set flying a cold roar;
Pushing deep through weak vines,
　　where late blossoms still are hanging.
Reluctant to leave, again I view
　　a wall painting I once did;
Remembering coming then, I add a note
　　to my old signature.
In front of the gate you're back upon
　　the road to the Red Dust realm:
Anyone willing to come join me here,
　　washing off vulgar hat-strings?   101

Bamboo, Xia Hui (1765–after 1829). Hanging
scroll, ink on silk, 26 ¼ x 19 in (67 x 48.2 cm). Hashi-
moto Collection exhibit at the Shoto Museum,
Tokyo, 1987.

108–112   *The River Residence of Degree-Holder Xia—*
              Five Poems

i *The Pavilion Pillowed on the Flow*

You love the beauty of this misty scene:
Studio's opened windows purposely overlook the stream.
Clear-sky brilliance beams on the cold waves;
Flying reflections shake on window paper.
Leaning on the railing seeing fish swim,
Rolling up the curtain, knowing geese take off:
Why so much grief?—You mock Qu Yuan's[81] burden
    by the Xiang,
So petty! Singing of "orchid" and "iris!"

ii *The Pavilion of Competing Azures*

After the rain, mountain scenes so fresh;
Wind once settled down, river brilliance fine.
Clear-sky sunlight breaks up last night's fog;
Gorgeous colors so thick you could sweep them along.
In peaceful times, a jug of wine,
And rustic guests to drain it with you.
Morning, evening among these mountains and rivers,
You know nothing of aging with the passing years.

---

81   The final couplet mentions iconic poet Qu Yuan (4th century. BC), who was unfairly exiled for political reasons, and in his poems complained of people's failure to recognize his purity and excellence, associating himself with "orchid" and other flowers and plants emblematic of noble purity. Eventually he committed suicide by drowning himself in a river. The Degree-Holder, like the fisherman in one of the poems linked to the Qu Yuan story, berates Qu for his unbending and self-destructive self-righteousness.

iii *The Cave Where a Heaven is Hidden*

Layered cliffs, sliced to reveal greenish gemstone:
Who was it in the past who drilled and sculpted here?
So dark and deep, they exposed this lone cave,
With space aplenty for a hundred men!
Towering peaks, linked mountains all around,
And raging Yangtze torrent splashing in!
When Yu Qing[82] wished to write his book,
He came here: how many years did he take?

iv *The Jetty of the Straight Fishing Hook*

We all know human hooks are crooked,
We only see your hook to be quite straight.[83]
Year after year, here on this jetty,
With ten thousand tries, not one catch so far!
Holding the rod, you've experienced just frustration;
Nibbles on the bait? When has that occurred?
Why don't you try what everyone else is doing?
You'll have fish galore, more than you can eat.

v *The Retreat for Getting Drunk on the Classics*

You hung some thatch, wove it into a retreat:
Something like a yurt in its construction.
And this man—yourself—huddles there, within,
Saying you're getting drunk on all the classics!
How could the vulgar of the world grasp what you're doing?
All they can say is, you're never really sober.
But let's send word to the two types of bravos:
This man is nothing like your Liu Ling![84]

DYJ 10/1b-2b; no. ii in *Anthology* 115

---

82 Yu Qing was a famed strategist of antiquity who wrote a book modeled on the *Spring and Autumn Annals* of Confucius, commenting on history.
83 The metaphor is clear: the only way to get ahead in this world is to set aside straight honesty for crooked duplicity.
84 The last couplet refers to Liu Ling, one of the most famous drunkards of all time; in his "Ode in Praise of Wine," he spoke of officials and retired scholars as two types of heroic drinkers.

113   *Sick and Tired of Bugs*

The moon comes out, the pine-embankment shines;
Dew is falling, lotus-pond purified.
Tonight the weather so extremely fine,
Alone I stroll around, all through the wood.
But—what are you up to, you hundred types of bugs?
Za-Za-Za . . . so full of autumn noise!
I'm seeking quiet, but I cannot find it:
How will I ever finish up this poem?   116

114–115   *What a Laugh!—Improvised, Seven Poems*[85]

iii

What a laugh! This old boy
   is so very stupid—
Reading books, practicing calligraphy
   right up to midnight!
Of course I know excessive study's
   not much use at all,
But—I'm determined to work as hard
   as those born after me.

vii

What a laugh! In mountain village
   to serve as an official,
Slow and quiet, not at all
   like bustling river town.
If only it weren't for all these books
   and paintings I must finish,
My hair would not be turning white
   as quickly as it is.   118–119

---

85   Two of the seven are translated here.

116 *Non-Action Mountain Temple*

Rope-like, the tricky path
    winds round the towering peaks,
On top, penetrating the hidden depths
    to enter the "City of Transformation."
The streams and plains beyond the mist:
    who embroidered them into this picture?
The towers and pavilions among the clouds
    have their "cloudy" and "clear."
The exalted discourse of these monks
    has never been written down;
The True Body of the ancient Buddha
    looks just as if alive.
I hear a general has taken away
    newly blessed holy water:
"I wonder if you could pour a few drops for me
    to wash my dusty hat-strings?"[86]   *DYJ*, 9/5b

---

86 As in poems 12 and 107, the "hat-strings" are used to tie in place the special cap worn by officials. The phrase thus becomes a common synechdoche for official garb, and by extension the life of an official.

117   *Reading Yuanming's*[87] *Collected Works*

The clerks have gone home,
    the office is completely quiet;
Business ended now,
    ears, eyes purified . . .
Through the windows, a lovely breeze,
    no vulgar guests at all;
And of books left on my desk,
    there is only yours, dear sir.
Writing of such pith and simplicity—
    yea, robe of emperors;
Flavor pure, yet rich as well—
    the Sacrificial Broth,
I eagerly await the time
    when, like you, I'll "Go Home."
But—what to do when this sagely era
    is such a time of peace?   *DYJ* 9/6a

118   *Staying Overnight at Longping Temple*

Ten thousand trees spread their verdant canopy;
Paired peaks unfold a blue-green screen.
Wind-blown dust grieves the traveler on his road,
While bell and drum gladden the Zen precincts.
Dismounting, I penetrate the heavy thickness,
Follow the monk-guide into the hidden mystery.
If my worldly garment may indeed be washed clean,
May they sprinkle me with *kundika*[88] aspersorium.   *DYJ* 9/6b

---

87 Here the poet complains tongue-in-cheek that since times are good, rather than troubled as in the time of Tao Yuanming (see note 2), he must follow the Confucian way of serving, rather than retiring.

88 *Kundika* is Sanskrit for a water vessel used for holding and sprinkling holy water in Buddhism. It is important in the iconography of one of the most widespread forms of the Bodhisattva Guanyin, who comes to the aid of mortals in distress.

119   *West Lake*

In this place, where Prime Ministers have lingered,
Glory burgeons with sunset.
The lake preserves the ancient dream;
The city laments the tragedies of the past.
Mists and vapors emerge here, cloudy or clear;
Ducks and gulls come home here, from far away, or near.
The wind through the pines seems to have a purpose:
It still wants to become music for the zither's golden stops.[89]

DYJ 9/7a

120   *At the Mid-Autumn Festival, Facing the Moon—*
       Thinking of Daoist Deng of Phoenix Mountain,
       I Send This to Him

There is a wanderer out there, among a thousand cliffs
        and ten thousand gullies:
Green hair, cinnabar face,
        and purple, squarish pupils![90]
I don't know, tonight,
        beneath the moon of the western tower,
Where on earth this flying immortal
        is descending from the bluish void?   *DYJ* 9/7b–8a

---

89   The final couplet implies that, just as the glories and tragedies of past events in this region have been sung in music and poetry, the place still wishes to become the stuff of art.

90   The seemingly bizarre appearance of the man is entirely consistent with features that appear on the person of one who has attained longevity or immortality through the various methods of Daoist religious practice, including concocting the elixir of immortality from cinnabar and other ingredients, special breathing exercises, and imbibing certain efficacious herbs.

121   *Late Clearing on a Day in Autumn—*
       Presented to a Fellow Official

> The autumn wind sighs and hisses,
>   blowing across the blue void;
> White clouds are arranged in scales,
>   like an enormous fish up there.
> Tonight, together with you, I will enjoy
>   the brilliant moon:
> Should inspiration strike, who wants to take
>   a ride on the Moon-Frog?[91]   *DJY* 9/8a

122   *Ziping Lost Tea and Ink to Me in a Game of Chess:*
       With this Little Poem I Take him to Task

> Sleeping, I remembered you pouring out
>   the bubbling goodness of Fujian tea;
> Painting? I think of how you splashed
>   ink from Yan in profusion!
> But now, alas, these two treasures
>   no longer are around:
> As I recall, I won them at the Southern Hall
>   when I beat you at chess!   *DYJ* 9/8b

123–126   *An Additional Four Poems on Blue Citadel*
           Mountain[92]

i *The Shrine of Brilliant Blessings*

> Bejeweled cliffs spiral up to the Jade Empyrean;
> Shades of blue-green shift with every step.
> Such clouds and mists could never be painted;
> Such streams and rocks—can't find in any book.

---

91   The Moon-Frog is one of several entities said to live in the moon.

92   Blue Citadel Mountain (Qingcheng shan) is associated with Daoist religious prac-
tices. In spite of the title there are no other poems on the subject in the extant writings of
Wen Tong. The "precious plaques" would be inscribed with official certificates for those
who had received special Daoist training.

Spirit-banners, more than a hundred feet long!
Traces of visiting Heavenly Lords from high antiquity.
Who could reach the source of the divine waterfall?
It flies out wide, bringing rain morning, noon, and night.

ii *The Shrine of Solemn Dignity at Heavenly Granary Mountain*

Clustered peaks cut to sheer gemstone cliffs;
Old lichens mottle them with ancient green.
They must be en route to pay court to Great Min Mountain,
Hat-pins and scepters in orderly file as they go.
In the Pearl Palace are hidden Immortals' regalia;
Embroidered bookbags store the precious plaques.
The Lord on High takes this to be his storehouse;
The fields here are worthy of planting jade.

iii *The Temple Where Immortals Flock*

Level woods reveal layered mountains;
At the very summit is perched a solitary temple.
Entourages of Immortals, in soaring equipages
Often flock unto this place.
The winds blow strong—flag-shadows flutter wildly;
The sun sets—sounds of bells arise.
Who would be dubbed a Hero of Poetry?[93]
Struck by this inspiration, let him fill ten thousand sheets!

iv *The Temple of Accumulated Fragrance*

The way is treacherous, twisting and turning;
The deeper in, the more precipitous the slopes.
Walking past pines, ears and eyes are purified;
Entering bamboo, sleeves, lapels are chilled.
The halls, pavilions are red hibiscus;
The cliffs, peaks, blue-green gemstone bamboo.
A noble monk holds a *sutra* with gold characters:
Huddled in his cassock, he reads, up among the clouds.

DYJ 10/1a–b

---

93 The term Hero of Poetry has been used to designate the important Tang poet Liu
Yuxi (772–842), but that does not seem to be the intention here.

127–130   *Four Poems Sent to be Inscribed on the Official Residences of Assistant Sub-Prefect of Hangzhou, Scholar Hu*

i *Phoenix Beak Hall*

[*Poet's preface*] According to the book of the Grand Historian,[94] the official residence is located beneath Phoenix Mountain. This mountain is indeed shaped like a phoenix, with two wings and a pagoda built on each wing, while the phoenix's bill happens to fall precisely above the pond of the residence. In the old days, there was a hall on the mountain, just above the place where the bill would touch down. This recently has been renovated, and named Phoenix Beak Hall, and a poem about it has been requested.

> Master Hu,[95] Assistant Sub-Prefect,
>   has come to Hangzhou,
> And the mountain where he takes up residence
>   is named Phoenix Mountain.

> We don't know the ultimate source of this name,
> But serpentine neck and fish-like tail
>   coil round the high ridges.
> With delicate movement it seems to descend
>   to drink from the great river;

---

94   The book mentioned likely does not refer to the classic *Shiji* (*Records of the Historian*) of Sima Qian, but perhaps to some more recent historical work or more likely a gazetteer of Hangzhou.

95   Jia Chengzhi, the Southern Song editor of Wen Tong's works (his colophon dated 1195), added prose notes in which he puts forth the controversial theory that "Master Hu" is in fact a reference to "Zizhan," or Su Shi; he later makes a similar claim about the name "Ziping." After the lengthy poet's note to this first poem he writes: "These four poems were written for Zizhan. Here he [Wen] has changed his [Su's] name to Master Hu. Is it perhaps the case that the disaster of the [Yuanyou] faction had not yet been fully dissipated, and so he made this revision, thus avoiding the truth?" In other words, any indication of closeness to Su Shi might implicate Wen Tong or his family members (who might have pressured him to suppress Su Shi's actual names) in the downfall of the Yuanyu-period (1086–1093) faction to which Su Shi belonged and thus resulted in trouble for them. (Political factionalism of this sort, resulting in the exile of the "losing" parties, was endemic to the traditional Chinese system of civil service.)

It sighs a single breath—ten thousand miles!—
    head lowering, then raised.
Who placed pagodas there,
    pressing down its two wings?
As if it were weighted to the ground,
    unable to soar on high!
In the past, people of vulgar vision
    did not know how to view it,
But then came a sagely man
    who grasped its physiognomy.

[*Here the poet addresses the mountain directly*]

"Loving you, he wished to converse with you,
And so, right beside your beak!—he had this hall constructed.
Now, active or resting, drinking or dining,
    he never parts from you—
In the outside world, who has the ear
    to hear your gemlike voice?
We must conclude that your virtue-power
    still lives, not yet declined:
Morning and evening, you might yet arise,
    and sing to the morning light."

In a note to the title of poem four, "Moon-Cliff Studio," Jia adds, "The name Ziping in this poem is in fact Zizhan." Modern Su Shi authority Kong Fanli has questioned at least the claim about the name Ziping, as it appears as a "courtesy name" for Su Shi only in Wen Tong's writings. Also, this Ziping holds offices never held by Su Shi. Finally, it has been claimed that Wen Tong had a friend, Su Jun 蘇鈞, with the courtesy name Ziping, who is actually being referred to. Kong must be right about Ziping, but the question of the cognomen "Master Hu" must probably await further research (see www.yuwenonline.com).

ii *The Studio that Sprays Jade-Drops*

[*Poet's preface*] The book [of the Grand Historian] further states that on the mountain, and among the brush and grasses are found many fantastic rocks. Recently, they have obtained over one hundred examples, and placed them in the Eastern Studio garden, where they have been used to construct a "mountain" with spurting water emerging from it. This is now called, The Studio that Sprays Jade-Drops.

> Forest of rocks—ancient trees—
> > deployed at the corner of the house;
> Spurting waters, splashing, shooting,
> > fly down stone canals.
> The cold symphony chimes out loud,
> > descends to form circled gems;
> Brisk, wafted air with sighing sounds
> > arises from the courtyard.
> The master's exemplary character
> > just maybe might be matched,
> But what lovely sites in which locale
> > could possibly equal these?
> I imagine, sir, you'd never wish
> > to part from here one moment:
> What else is there? A desk piled high
> > with files and documents.

iii *The Square Hermitage*

[*Poet's preface*] The book further states that behind the main hall there is a hut which is precisely square, and is called The Square Hermitage. I, [Wen] Tong, would note that according to the *Shiming*[96] the word *an* 庵 etymologically means a "round hut."

> People's huts are all of them *round*;
> Your hut alone is called "Square!"
> Although you seem quite content therein,
> Is this not being a bit too eccentric?
> I'd urge you to lop off the corners,
> And then perhaps rename it, "Bed to rest the moon."

---

96   The *Shiming*, or *Explication of Names*, is an early dictionary dating from ca. AD 200.

Quite naturally, the structure would be stable,
And the name as well would withstand scrutiny.
East, West, South, North—
    no need to distinguish!
Left, Right, Front, Back—
    who could take offense?
I wish for your seeing and hearing
    both to be like this:
Then folks would fear injuring even rats and scorpions
    in all four directions.[97]

iv *Moon-Cliff Studio*[98]

[*Poet's preface*] The book further states that they piled up rocks to make a "mountain," and on it was one "peak" pierced through with an opening shaped like the moon, hence they called the place Moon-Cliff Studio.

The moon is the quintessence of the Supreme *Yin* Force;
Rocks too are of the moon's ilk.
The moon routinely is born in wombs of stone:
Such being the Principles of things
    why should we be surprised?
When Heaven and Earth were first divided,
The Sun and Moon appeared, each a separate thing.
And since they had *names*, they now entered *forms*,
But how could "form" forever not be changed?
What is more, this Sun and Moon

---

97   The last line might mean that the roundness of the hermitage would generate such a feeling of harmony that a "peaceable kingdom" would result, in which people would avoid harming even noxious creatures such as rats and scorpions.

98   This extraordinary tour de force, somewhat in the manner of Li Bai (or Li Po, 701–762) on one level is an energetic parody of pedantry, almost reminding one of Pope's mock-epic mode, and written entirely tongue-in-cheek. The allusions are too many to elucidate fully, but Nü Wa, for example, famously patched the sky with rocks when it was damaged by the depredations of another demi-god, rejecting poor rocks and casting them aside. The intimate relationship between rocks, mountains, and meteorological phenomena is well established in Chinese lore. It must also be kept in mind that the whole poem describes what is in fact a "miniature mountain" or "fantastic rock" shaped like a mountain and placed in a garden. The 82,000 craftsmen(!) are first mentioned in a book of miscellaneous matters factual and fictional, *Youyang zazu* (*Miscellaneous Offerings on the Sacrificial Table from Youyang*), attributed traditionally to Duan Chengshi (mid-9th century), but the authenticity of which has been questioned.

Morning and night travel between east and west.
A pearl flowing, a jade-disc turning—never stopping a moment—
How could they last as long as Heaven and Earth?
That both bodies have painstaking labors everybody knows,
The moon with fixed times of birth and death.
This being so, they must forever change their forms,
But we humans cannot see what the gods perform.
The sun must be born up in the sky;
The moon must be produced from deep within the earth.
Sir, do you not see:
 Among mountains and valleys of Zhuyang in Guozhou,
The moon forms there but while not yet complete,
 how can we know what limits its growth?
Perhaps some stone is lacking in quality:
Yet often the "egg" hatches therein!
The Divine Lady, Nü Wa, rejects it, and pays no further heed,
Allowing people to collect it and turn it into a treasure.
The lovely ones they keep, against Heaven's taking it back;
Filling storehouses and coffers with them,
 hundreds of thousands and more!
Yanzhan's *Encyclopedia*, praised as the *ne plus ultra* by the world,
Certainly would not consider my theory to be mere dream-talk—
In fact, I fear the people of this world
 don't realize that in the grottoes of Sacred Mount Song
Reside 82,000 craftsmen, their job to *repair the moon!*
Their diet consists entirely of jade dust.
Once a certain young scholar Wang met with them,
 their bags filled with chisels and axes;
It must have been that at that time, Divine Vulture Mountain[99]
Flew straight from India, landing right on the banks of West Lake!
Upon it was a rock, already pregnant with the moon,
 the moon already full:
Could it be that one of the craftsmen came there,
  cut out the moon,
   and scuttled back up to Heaven?
And so this rock remained split, no longer whole as before?

---

99   Peak of the Divine Vulture, or Gijja-kūṭa Peak (as in the next poem), is where
Buddha once taught; it flew to China from India, and is located at West Lake

While to this day, the part where the divine womb was implanted
    has left a round-shaped gash?
Then it was cast off beside the road, for oh, how many years,
Wind-scoured, rain-soaked, dirtied by road-dust.
And then—Ziping saw it, a single glance, and he
    was deeply moved in his heart.
He had it transported by carriage to the Eastern Studio,
    washing it, polishing it himself;
And then he selected other rock-mountains
    to hug and accompany it,
But with this single peak right at the center,
    most wondrous of all!
And whenever some bejeweled phase of the moon
    sends beams flowing down so bright,
The jade columns slant and lean without the slightest flaw.
Now, Ziping considers me to share his interests,
And from ten thousand miles away
    he has sent me his writing on this.
He invites me to write a poem of my own, but . . .
    how could I possibly?
Before my window, for days on end now,
    I've stared at empty paper.
But still, from so far away, I picture the precious cave on the cliff,
    letting through the moonlight,
And the Jade Frog from this point on
    will disappear from the sky without a trace!
I beg you, sir, for my sake write
    tiny characters alongside the cave,
Naming this: *The Peak, Mother of the Moon.*   *DYJ* 10/1a–4b

131   *Seeing Off Wuyan on his Return to Chengdu*[100]

I once read the *Essay in Aid of the Teaching*
    by monk Qisong;[101]
From this I knew the religion of the Buddhists
    could not simply be ignored.
Later, in the capital, I met the monk
    Huailian;[102]
This noble religious, especially extraordinary!
I once in conversation asked him about his friends:
And Lian for me discussed another monk, his name, Ju'na.[103]
These three great men were gifted beyond others:
With this endowment, how could they be
    overawed by us Confucians?
Their writings overflowed with power, their moral tone so rich!
These were not of that ilk who serve their Buddha
    only in trivial ways.
When I contemplate monks on this level,
    who comes to mind as comparable to them?
—In Sichuan, it happens, there is one man
    who too is utterly transcendent!
He is Minxing of Chengdu City,
    courtesy name, Wuyan,
Of him it might be said he is the Moon
    among ten thousand mere satellites.

---

100 An extremely eloquent and detailed eulogy of a friend who was indeed one of the foremost Buddhist monks of his time. When the poet apparently urges his friend to leave the monastic life and enter government service, the tone is probably playful, although there certainly are examples of monks returning to a lay life. The poem may be seen as an apologia for Wen's serious interest in Buddhism, a kind of spiritual autobiography. The departure of Minxing here described took place in 1073. See prose no. 8.

101 Qisong (1007–1072) was one of the great monks of Wen Tong's day. For an important, recent study of him, see Elizabeth Morrison, *Power of Patriarchs: Qisong and Lineage in Chinese Buddhism* (Leiden: Brill Academic Publishers, 2010).

102 For Huailian, another important monk of the day, see Chang Bide, et al, *Songren zhuanji ziliao suoyin*, Vol. 5, p. 4481; and Li E, *Songshi jishi*, ch. 91, pp. 2186–87, which gives a poem of his presented to Emperor Renzong (r. 1023–1063) requesting that he be allowed to leave the capital and return to his temple after he had been honored by a summons to the court.

103 For Ju'na (1010–1071), an associate of fellow-monk Huailian, see Chang Bide, op. cit., Vol. 5, p. 4403.

I imagine Song, Lian, and Na meeting him,
    and deferring to him right away!
Otherwise, they'd be repeatedly *shooed* away by him!
He comprehends Chan meditation, grasps Vinaya rules,
    both mastered without the slightest flaw;
In a former life he must have attended gatherings
    at Gijja-kūṭa Peak!
The Classics? The Histories?
    His knowledge encompasses the whole field;
He has explored their greatest depths,
    swimming effortlessly among them.
As for sidelines, what he is excellent at doing
    is calligraphy and painting:
But he never discusses these at all—ask and he'll merely stutter!
Reckoning up his summers and winters,
    they're actually not that many,
Yet in the masses of men,
    he stands utterly alone.
When I was governing Lingyang,
    I lived in poverty;
Rains soaked the place for an entire springtime,
    and I was swimming in mud.
Ying Stream impassable with rocks,
    stone-strewn paths so treacherous,
Visitors would pant and wheeze
    trying to ascend the precipitous cliffs,
But Wuyan? He alone braved the danger,
    without the slightest concern,
Appeared, knocked on my door,
    and presented his visiting card!
His physiognomy was vibrant, full,
    hiding within divine bone-structure.

[*Poet's note*] The poem by Tuizhi [Han Yu, 768–824] "Seeing Off Cheng'guan" has this line: "Seated, I observe his divine bone-structure, as he weeps for no apparent reason."

In Pure Conversation we sat there long,
    and he seemed still more fresh and free.
Suddenly, dust fell from my robe
    as if he had brushed it away;
And his new poems, his ancient-style prose—
    examining these marvelous gifts,
I saw his style was powerful, liberated,
    like the flight of the frost-piercing falcon!
And when I heard the fluent flow
    of his doctrinal exposition
I knew such dignity could take its place
    among hat-pins and scepters of state,
And so I actually invited him
    to pursue an official career!
But, laughing, and pointing to his head: "How could this
    bald pate
    ever again grow hair?"
Daily did I invite him, never tiring
    of having such converse with him,
But how could I know he'd announce his departure
    so unexpectedly?
From the western city-wall, dawn sunbeams
    illuminating towering ridges,
His saffron robe, as if fading,
    disappears into forest shade.
As the Master returns, may he always be blessed
    by auspicious protection;
The mind of this venerable
    is already without worldly taint.
"May you favor me often with excellent news:
Here in this deserted mountain,
    I'm lonely and depressed."   *DYJ* 10/5b–6b

132   *The Investigator has Given me the Gift of Li Shuzi's Seal*
      Calligraphy from E'zhou

There is wondrous seal calligraphy in this world,
Done by Li Yangbing at E'zhou.
Weird beasts yawning wide their five mouths;
Crazy Bites[104] shaking all three of their heads!
Piled blocks like crystalline bowls,
Twisting, writhing like coral hooks!
I'm ashamed not to have a world-class treasure
To exchange with you for this rare gift.   *DYJ* 10/8a

133   *For Two Years the Mid-Autumn Moon Has not Been*
      Visible at Lingyang

At Lingyang, among the wild mountains,
Dark vapors issue, morning, noon, and night.
Clear-sky daylight is rarely seen;
How much the less the moon at night?
For two years now, Mid-Autumn's come around,
And not for a moment have we known the brilliant beams.
"Mist and cloud! What is the reason
You always draw your layers of fog at this time?
Just as you've allowed some light where the veil is thin,
You send a heavy patch to sink the disc!"
Evil forces profit from this deep darkness:
We've heard susurrating, whispering, to left and right.
Should the pure light stay misted this way,
Won't anyone wipe the haze away for me?
In the courtyard, I lean against a tall tree,
Dew drops moistening sideburns and hair. *DYJ* 11/1a

---

104 Crazy Bites are apparently Cerberus-like monsters, possibly invented by the poet.
Li Yangbing (fl. 8th century.) is the most famous master of archaic "seal calligraphy." The
gift in this case would have been a rubbing taken from a rock-cut inscription.

134   *Night Sounds*

Autumn wind rustles withered flora,
Sighing soughing, echoes rising to the night moon.
Below, there are chirping cicadas,
Singing without cease until the light of dawn.
And so I realize at this season of falling leaves,
All nature's voices are naturally moved to cry.
So why is it that the poet of suffering
Cannot produce even a single sob?   *DYJ*, 11/1a–b

135   *Seeing Off the "Chess Monk," Weizhao*

You've mastered the *Nine Chapters*,[105]
        the secrets of higher equations;
You recite from memory monk Yixing's
        poems on multiplication and division.
With such natural genius,
        you understand this supreme art:
You could match any National Master—
        you must become my teacher!
There, where you huddle by the brazier
        on the bench beside the window,
Just when outside, a great snowfall
        presses down upon the roof,
Alone, you replay an old game,
        analyzing the errors
With a cold laugh at the ancients!
        To whom might you ever concede?   *DYJ* 11/1b

---

105 The *Nine Chapters* is an abbreviation for *Jiu zhang suan shu* (*Mathematical Techniques in Nine Chapters*) described by Joseph Needham as "perhaps the most important of all Chinese mathematical books." In its current form it is most likely of Han dynasty date, but including earlier material (see Joseph Needham with Wang Ling, *Science and Civilisation in China,* Cambridge University Press, 1959, Vol. 3, pp. 24–25; for "higher equations," see p. 123.) Buddhist monk Yixing (683—727), was a brilliant mathematician and calendrical expert. According to Shen Gua (or Guo, 1031–1095), "The storytellers say that I-Hsing [Yixing] once calculated the total number of possible situations, *ju* (局, the same word used by Wen Tong in the penultimate line of his poem, here translated "game") in chess, and found he could exhaust [i.e., master] them all" (cited in Needham and Ling, Vol. 3, p. 139).

136   *Sitting at Night on the Mid-Autumn Festival—*
      Expressing my Feelings

White silk fan not moved at all—yet wind-puffs fill my robe;
Moist dew-drops at midnight too invade me with their chill.
My feelings soar, but there's no way to send them in the dark:
They'd go with the moon, straight to the center of the sky.

DYJ 11/4a

137   *Rustic Path*

The mountain garden is wrapped in autumn colors;
Forest pavilions, clear-skies as evening comes.
The birds and creatures follow "Monthly Ordinances;"[106]
The medicinal herbs are named for famous men.
Arranging rocks, I spread my robe, take a seat;
Gazing at clouds, loosen my belt and wander.
Official duties done, such is my pleasure:
I wish to have no business with the outside world.

DYJ 11/4a–b

---

106 One chapter of the classic *Zhou li,* or *Rites of the Zhou Dynasty,* is devoted to the "Monthly Ordinances," that is, descriptions of the important signs of each season, as in the European "Occupations of the Months."

138   *In the year* xinhai [1071], *first month of autumn, on the
day wuzi, there appeared a rainbow,*[107] *descending from
the sky to embrace Flying Waterfall Mountain and enter
East Valley as if drinking from Ancient Well. After a long
time it disappeared, bringing in its wake a great rainfall.
Amazed by this, I wrote this poem.*

A long rainbow hung from heaven, a great sash:
Ten thousand leagues long, cutting off the clustered ridges.
With arching body it descended to the deep valley;
Dipping its head, it drank from Ancient Well.
The local people dared not point at it,
Or even lift their heads to gaze.
With a sudden flip, it disappeared from the sky,
Instantaneously transforming into cloud and fog.
Because of this, Heaven and Earth turned black,
Spewing forth rain with ferocious violence!
The crushing downpour filled canals with waves,
A vast swell inundating all four directions.
The farmers' fields were completely flooded,
And the many crops became invisible.
The rainbow is classified as "reptilian":
I have heard it even has neck and head!
Born of impure exhalations,
Recorded in the *Book of Songs* as a sign of catastrophe.

---

107 The rainbow was seen in China as an evil omen, and the idea that it was a living crea-
ture with serpentine features appears also to be uniquely Chinese. As Wen states, poem
51 of the *Book of Songs* opens as follows (as translated by Karlgren): "The rainbow is in
the east,/Nobody dares to point to it." This is paralleled with the account of a girl leaving
father, mother, and brothers, and going far away where she presumably enters into an
illicit relationship with a man rather than the marriage she had hoped for. Arthur Waley
writes that the "appearance" of the "rainbow . . . announces that someone who ought
not to is about to have a baby." He further notes that "[n]o one dares point at it, because
pointing is disrespectful, and one must respect a warning sent by Heaven." Wen uses the
phrase *mo zhi zhi* (莫之指, literally, "no one pointed at it") based on the "The Rainbow is
in the East" from *Book of Songs* 51:2: *mo zhi gan zhi* (莫之敢指, "No one dared to point
at it"). See Bernhard Karlgren, *The Book of Odes* (Stockholm: The Museum of Far Eastern
Antiquities, 1950), pp. 33–34; Arthur Waley, *The Book of Songs* (Grove Press reprint of
1937 publication), p. 61 (as his poem 64).

In the morning in the west, in the evening east it appears:
Casting shadows opposite to the sun's!
And why should this evil omen
Be allowed to present itself thus at will?
A high wind now wipes clean the whole panorama,
One single sweep, and dusky filthiness is obliterated!
Scintillating, brilliant, the great sun arises,
And every hole and crevasse is filled with sparkling light.
May every dark force be pursued into the ocean:
This creature must be imprisoned, far, far away!   *DYJ* 11/4b–5a

139 *Sending Some Pills Compounded of the Herb He Shouwu*[108] *to Friends*

This herb has marvelous effects!
I learned them first from Xizhi.
Lingyang too has produced it for ages,
The soil here being particularly suited to its growth.
Its blue-green vines spread across cliff-walls,
In fragrant clumps it shows luxuriant, uneven patterns.
Below are roots like fists,
Red and white distinguishing the male and female.
If you cut some after the height of autumn,
Its essence and fragrance will not fade.
Slice through with a machete for bitter-bamboo,
Steam and sun it through nine phases in all.
Wrap it in fine netting: fragrant particles will precipitate out,
And among closely clustered rocks
    these will blend with each other.
Introduce this mixture into a pestle,
    pound with mortar ten thousand times;
They will then fill a dish, rolling around in clusters.
Imbibe them as the days advance,
    don't worry about taking too many:

---

108 *He Shouwu* (何首烏) is an herb, literally "Blackhead He," *Fallopia multiflora*. In Daoist religious lore, there is a great emphasis on herbs considered to possess powers of longevity or even immortality, if prepared in accordance with special prescriptions. Some, like this one, are real; others are entirely mythical. Xizhi is the Tang philosopher Li Ao (772–841), author of "A Record of the He Shouwu Herb" (*He Shouwu lu*), which recounts how a man later nicknamed Shouwu (Blackhead) discovered this elixir of youth in the mountains. Wen Tong places his faith in Li Ao's account of the medicinal properties of the herb, which are real, but the herb is mistakenly considered by the masses to be a lowly weed, as opposed to one called *Xianlingbi* (仙靈毗, *Epimedium brevicornum Maxim*), which poet and prose writer Liu Zihou (Liu Zongyuan, 773–819) planted in his garden and praised in a poem. See Liu's collected works, *Liu Hedong ji*, in two volumes (Shanghai renmin chubanshe, 1974, vol. II, pp. 727–8). Liu also lays claim to esoteric knowledge of how to extract medicinal usefulness from the herb.

Li Ao's herb is still claimed today by herbal medicine authorities to have "rejuvenating effects on the nerves, brain cells, and endocrine glands," while Liu's is said to contain the active ingredient in Viagra! Note that both writers are concerned, like Wen, to communicate the proper technique for extracting the active ingredients from the herbs, as opposed to simply imbibing them as-is.

At first, they won't seem to have any benefit.
But after some time, you will feel your skin transform,
Becoming fresh and moist like congealed lard.
And next, your whiskers and hair will change:
There will not be a single white one left!
Your ears and eyes will certainly improve their hearing and vision,
And as for walking, you'll almost be running along!
Friends of mine, parted from me for ten years,
Suddenly saw me and were all puzzled and amazed;
They asked me, "How did you acquire these techniques
So that you look like a man who has never aged a bit?"
For their benefit, I expounded the virtues of this divine herb,
Unbeknownst to the vulgar of this world.
For this plant being plentiful is quite cheap,
And is consigned to the same low class as brambles and sticks.
"If you are persuaded by what you've heard,
I assure you, these statements will never prove a cheat.
Don't place your faith in Liu Zihou
Who merely boasts of the Immortals' Divine Barrenwort."

DYJ 11/5a–b

140   *The Fuchun Mountain Man has told me about a rock
he acquired from the river, extremely weird and majestic
in form. He wants me to write a poem about it, saying
that if he could obtain such a work, he would bring
it home and have it engraved on the rock so that this
text would last as long as the rock itself. I sat down at
night in the Pavilion Level with the Clouds, at a time
when the mountain moon was clear and cold, and the
chirping insects were singing in their most mournful
manner. Because of these surroundings, I sought out brush
and inkstone and composed a poem about this for the
Mountain Man.*

This fantastic boulder towered high
    beside the autumn river,
Vulgar eyes how many times
    simply ignoring it?
Wind and frost worked away at it,
    so it became even harder;
Angry waves spewed water on it—
    unsinkable as it was.
The Mountain Man of Fuchun Mountain
    is one who loves antiquity,
He took one look at it and thought,
    "This must become my own!"
He excavated it, tugged it home,
    placed it in his courtyard,
Like a rhinoceros horn, a whale tooth,
    or the skeleton of a kraken.
Essence of gold congealed to smooth surface,
    exposing sinew and spine;
Ancient jade piled into a structure
    pierced with grottoes and whorls.
A wild dragon rushing, clutching
    with youthful energy;
A ferocious rhino leading royal troops,
    with stupendous speed and force.

The Mountain Man, boasting to me,
    described it in this way,
As if he wanted my poem to be
    a shameful, clumsy offering![109]
When will I travel to the Mountain Man's home,
And see this rock jutting up,
    caressing the moon, brushing the mist?   *DYJ* 11/6a

141   *Hearing that Mountain Man Chen Dingming has
Successfully Refined the Elixir, I Attempt to Request
Some by Means of this Poem*[110]

Ice and Charcoal harmonized,
    you've nurtured the Great Return;
And I've heard the divine Mercury
    now fills your cauldron, dried!
Swine-fat and Lacquer-juice
    are easily obtained:
I dare to take the Spiritual Elixir—
    twenty thousand pills!   *DYJ* 11/6b

---

109 The idea expressed in the penultimate couplet seems to be that the Mountain Man's own images for the rock are grandiose and overblown, while Wen wants to write elegantly. The tone throughout is playful, with Wen gently making fun of the man who requested him to write.

110 This entire poem is composed of technical terms from Daoist alchemy. The Great Return of the first line refers to the completed cycle refining the Elixir, which involves bringing together or "harmonizing" apparent irreconcilables in nature, such as Ice and Charcoal (manifestations of the elements Water and Fire), leading to the extraction of the Mercury-based essence, no longer in liquid form but now in a dry state. According to the biography of a certain Li Baozhen in the *New History of the Tang Dynasty*, which had recently been compiled by Ouyang Xiu (1007–72) and a cohort of scholars, "There was a man named Sun Jizhang who was engaged in concocting the Elixir. He stated, 'Imbibe this, and you will certainly rise as an Immortal'. . . Baozhen imbibed 20,000 of the pills, but found them indigestible, and was on the very brink of death, but when doctored with Swine-fat and Lacquer-juice, he was able to digest them."

    Ordinarily, of course, lacquer would be toxic. But in alchemy the idea is that everything harmful is rendered beneficial. NB: My translation, Lacquer-juice, renders Wen's *guqi* 穀漆 (the character *gu* 谷 can substitute for *gu* 穀, meaning "grain"). My interpretation of the phrase is tentative.

142   *Among the Farmers—Autumn Days*

Washing out irrigation canals,
    they build a rustic tank;
Filling the slopes, misty grasses,
    reclining oxen, sheep.
This year they take pleasure: "We'll be able
    to afford our taxes!
Beanpods especially flourishing,
    grain-ears growing long!"   *DYJ* 11/7a–b

143   *The Old Man of East Hill*

The Old Man of East Hill
    has eyebrows bushy, long;
His flesh and skin aglow with health,
    his teeth firmly in place.
He says himself, "On New Year's
    I turned ninety-nine years old;
Whiskers? Hairs? Not one of them
    is white in color now!"
I question him: "Oh, my 'technique'?
    is really nothing at all:
Swallowing Saliva and In-taking Breath
    just make a lot a noise!
I don't let my Primal Energy
    be controlled by joy or sorrow,
And what I've gotten from this all naturally
    is—many springs and autumns.
I've been practicing it now
    for fifty years all told:
This 'technique' is easy indeed,
    and has never caused me any hardship at all."
I gave the man a few drinks of wine,
    and then sent him on his way;
As he departed, his arms and legs
    were strong and flexible in movement as those of any monkey!

I have read in the past of a man of the Tang dynasty,
    Liu Gongdu[111] by name:
At the age of over eighty, his vitality and strength
    were those of a young man,
And his explanation to others was similar
    to that of this old man:
Is it not possible that this old man
    is of that very same ilk?   *DYJ* 12/4a–b

144   *Remembering a Past Excursion to West Lake*

West Lake, clear-skies, blue—
    rippling calmly with evening:
Together with a friend, I came there,
    and sat in the lovely breeze.
I remember one time, someone was singing
    the song on Little Jade,[112]
The moonlight then still beaming on
    that painted boat of ours . . .   *DYJ*, 12/8b

---

111 The biography of Liu Gongdu's cousin, Liu Gongchuo, in the original *History of the Tang Dynasty* (which Ouyang's *New History* was intended to replace) states that Gongdu "was expert at Nurturing Life. When he was over eighty, he was still healthy and strong. He would often state, 'I have never had any 'technique'; it is simply that I have never allowed my 'Energy Ocean' to be warmed or chilled by external things, or by things either cooked or raw, nor have I allowed this Primal Energy to be controlled by joy or sorrow.'" The rhetorical force [logic?] of the final line in Wen's poem is that the current "old man," completely unknown, is certainly at least the equal of a man who was considered worthy to be recorded in one of the official histories.

112 The name of a famous singing girl.

145   *Mountain Garden*

Long rains—and nothing pleasant here;
New clearing, I walk the mountain garden.
West winds fill the tall trees,
Falling leaves—amazed they change so soon!
If seasons pass as fast as this,
What can we say of worldly affairs?
I return at night, chant poems in lamplight,
Cold insects accompany my solitary moan.   *DYJ* 12/9b

146   *I was Promised some River-Pig Fish*[113] *by Assistant Collector Shi but Have not yet Received Them: Making Fun of him in a Poem*

Frost-fall heavy, waters recede,
    ice along the shores:
The River-Pig enjoys the cold,
    comes out to play in sunlight.
Splashing waves, slapping ripples,
    suddenly—whole schools!
Thick their tails, long their mouths,
    fins all red in color.
The fishermen on such clear mornings
    embark in their big boats,
One throw of their enormous net,
    how many heads now caught?
I suspect your chopsticks now
    are tired of eating so many:
How about sending a few of them
    to me here at Lingzhou?   *DYJ* 12/9b–10a

---

113 The "river-pig" is the blowfish, still eaten in China and enormously popular in Japan, where special licenses are issued to blowfish chefs since, if not prepared properly, the fish can be fatally toxic. For this reason, poet and friend of Ouyang Xiu, Mei Yaochen (1002–1060) had used it as a symbol of factionalism (*dang*). Here, this aspect plays no role and the fish is simply a delicacy.

147   *Yellow Cliff Cave*

The great Cave of Yellow Cliff
    hides buried, ancient clouds;
Enter in and where you step
    is level like a mat.
Deeper in, the "jade marrow-bones"[114]
    are all quite edible,
I only worry that, once back home,
    you might turn into stone.   *DYJ* 12/10b

---

114 The "jade marrow-bones" are the stalactites and stalagmites.

148   *Ziping has sent me a gift, the Tangfu Mountain herb*[115]
      which was imbibed by Mr. Chen [Tuan] Xiyi[116] *with*
      instructions, so I have playfully written this poem in
      varied line-lengths to thank him.

Along the eastern bank of the River Shu,
    the mountains are all ochre-tinted;
A Daoist has told me what this means—
    cinnabar-sands hidden below.
The mist and cloud are brilliant and rich in moisture,
    as if washing the mountains;
The gulley-valleys are sparkling and clear, as if engraved
    into a picture.
And I have heard that the herbs of the divine Immortals
    never grow in ordinary soil,
So this region must certainly grow roots and stems
    of spiritual sprouts and extraordinary plants.
And sure enough, people say that the mountain taros that
    grow here are
        the finest in the world;
Those famous ones from the southwestern counties
    enjoy their reputation in vain.
Among these products, the Tangfu herb
    is highest praised of all;
Plump fruit, sweet fragrance—nurtured by very Heaven.
Sometimes from the tips of cliffs
    they hang down three feet in length
        like arms of mighty soldiers;
Or, suddenly, at the mouth of a cave,
    they will shoot straight up in a single cluster,
        like the palms of Immortals' hands.

---

115 I cannot identify the "Tangfu Mountain herb"(*Tangfushanyao*, 唐福山藥), or per-
haps"The herb of Mr. Tang Fushan."
116 The biography of Chen Tuan (ca. 920–989), the famous Daoist alchemist men-
tioned in the title, intermingles fact and fiction. For an excellent summation of what we
know of him, see the account by Livia Kohn in Fabrizio Pregadio, ed., *The Encyclopedia of
Taoism* (two volumes, Routledge, 2008, pp. 257–259). See also prose numbers 4 and 10.

The local farmers, when winter sets in,
    and farm chores are all done,
With a thousand baskets and ten thousand spades
    will come to this mountain;
Yet, alas, the price at which they sell the herb
    is not high at all:
These folks, in setting the price to sell,
    have never been greedy at all!
Two years back, Zizhan[117] explained to me:
"Of the products of the region where you now govern,
    this herb is by far the most marvelous!"
And later on, he also wrote to me, urging me
    for sure to imbibe this herb!
And he filled up sheets of paper, copying out
    Mr. Sacred Mount Hua's Secret Techniques.[118]
I therefore purchased some, not sparing any cash,
And, following the instructions, imbibed the herb
    going on two years now.
The effectiveness has been divinely sagely,
    felt now only after this long a time:
Sinews strong, body overflowing with energy,
    limbs and joints all powerful.
I ask myself, when will I be able to ascend
    to that Cinnabar Empyrean,
So I can, soon as possible, grow two wings,
    and thus to soar up high?
I am like a prisoner in this realm of dust,
    and can live here no longer:
I await the sight of Great Vastness,
    where I'll join the Cloud Generals![119]

                                        DYJ 12/11b–12a

---

117 Zizhan: If the theory of Jia Chengzhi is correct, and Wen Tong never used this, the actual courtesy name of Su Shi, substituting in its place "Ziping" (as in the title of this poem), this occurrence of Zizhan might be a mistake on the part of Wen himself, or it could be an editor's or copyist's error, going back to Jia Chengzhi himself or later.

118 *Mr. Sacred Mount Hua's Secret Techniques* would be a book of Daoist alchemical and herbal lore, or a mnemonic jingle of the same nature.

119 The last line refers to two immortals who play a role in the *Zhuangzi.*

149   *View of Hanchuan Beneath Clear Skies*

From city walls, watching the rain clear,
Heaven and Earth seem newly washed clean.
But toward evening, a change to clouds and haze,
Autumn feeling touching plants and trees.
The Four Seasons transform thus easily,
While life's ten thousand affairs press so bitterly.
When will I return to the old mountain home,
The three paths rich in chrysanthemums and pines?[120]   127

150   *A Summer Night*

The guest-house by the pond, desolate,
    drawing on to midnight;
The woods are full of insects, birds—
    not a chirp from them.
Wind blows down pine-cones
    with a sound like falling rain;
Moonlight shines on lotus blossoms,
    thick as banks of cloud.
The stream here forms a tiny rapids,
    rushing, gurgling sound;
Shoots are forming new bamboo,
    breathing vital force.
Shade purified—a perfect time
    to revisit "poetry-chanting rock,"
Where towering *wutong* trees
    will brush against my plain silk robe.   128

---

120 The last line conflates allusions to two iconic recluses of the past, Jiang Xu of the Han dynasty and the poet Tao Qian, or Tao Yuanming (365–427). See note 40.

151 *The Hall of Purified Scenes*

> After public duties, fewer dusty worries;
> In leisure does one see the truth of things.
> Canna blossoms, thick red torches!
> Bamboo knots, light rings of powder!
> Swallows moor on curtain hooks, and chatter;
> Bees[121] seek out the brush rack, as they buzz.
> Serene, I can know such epiphanies,
> And laugh—*Ha! Ha!*—at the life of useless toil.   128

152 *Evening Inspirations*

> The gang of clerks, dismissed for the day;
> The West Garden now, my favorite haunt!
> Last chess game covered, the moss-pavilion quiet;
> Herb-circulating walk,[122] far across the rope bridge.
> Grass colors perfect beneath clear skies
>   to show marks of my clogs;
> Pine shade, hidden, washes clean my robe.
> The "mountain-millipede!" Again I'm moved to write of it,
> Leaning on bamboo, I listen to its clear tones!   129

---

121 The bees are attracted by the smell of dripping ink, redolent of pine resin.
122 An "herb-circulating walk" would expedite the effect of any herbs imbibed; millipedes actually make sounds by rubbing their claws together.

153 *The Judicial Commissioner has Shown Me the* Painting
of Birds at Night,[123] *and I have Written this Poem to*
Sing of it

Red plum blossoms in profusion, showing through
  the sparse bamboo;
Cold trees all withered, covering
  a rustic jetty.
A great snowfall, obscuring the sky,
  descending in confusion,
And flocks of birds, contending for ground,
  all huddled there together. . .
Except for a connoisseur like yourself,
  who could have acquired this treasure?
Such paintings in this day and age
  have grown extremely rare.
Try waiting for spring's Pure-Bright Festival,
  and hang it from your study wall:
The birds will surely open their eyes,
  and all fly off together!   133

---

123 The proud owner of this painting was Wen Tong's fellow official and friend, Zhang
Jingru 張景孺. A painting of this name is attributed in various old catalogues to a
painter named Su Wen 蘇汶 of the earlier Song or Five Dynasties period (906–ca. 960),
of whom nothing further appears to be known. See poem 227 for another reference to
this painting.

154　*After Rain in the Northern Studio*

Hidden garden in a little courtyard,
　　the ultimate in pure beauty;
Loving it so much, I frequently order
　　early staff dismissal.
After rain, a pair of birds
　　descend, occupy bamboo;
Deep in autumn, just one butterfly
　　appears in search of flowers.
I call someone to brush off the dusty wall,
　　revealing a Wu Daozi painting,
Detain guests to enjoy the verandah view
　　and try a tea from Yue.[124]
These rustic pleasures keep increasing,
　　as public duties diminish,
Just like the old days, when I was residing
　　in my mountain home.　　　　　　　　134

---

124 Yue is an ancient name for Zhejiang Province, famous for several varieties of tea.

155–168   *Miscellaneous Poems on the Garden Buildings at Xingyuan Prefecture*

i *The Hall of Supreme Beauty*

Vast, magnificent in roof and beam,
Verandah windows opening on great mystery;
High and deep, suitable to the locale,
Perfect for holding a great banquet!
Should office duties slow down a bit,
Here I will gather elegant guests.

ii *The Wuling Studio*

The stream flows from the cliff out front,
And then into the creek behind.
And in a boat, wine on board and heading downstream,
They all come to join the other guests.
After intoxication, everyone's so muddled,
They'd never be able to find the place again.[125]

iii *The Pavilion of Verdant Scenery*

Amongst the bamboo, a hidden pavilion,
Uniquely right for drinking in summer heat.
Layers of shade protect from the flaming sun;
Guests on all four sides, screened by green embroidery.
But afternoon past, one cannot stay:
Wearing just light linen, it starts to feel a bit cold.

iv *The Pavilion of the Rushing Torrent*

High up, wheel-like it spins to the deep abyss,
Splashing down to the mouth of the Stone Moon-Frog!
Overlooking, they set up a verandah with railings,
Pure, supreme, without parallel anywhere.
Loving the spot, I come here to the mountains,
And then will always sit a long, long time.

---

125 This is a humorous variation on the story of the Wuling fisherman who stumbled upon the lost paradise, Peach Blossom Spring, and never could find it again.

v *The Gazebo of Congealed Cloud*

Morning clouds spit forth by the southern mountains,
Evening clouds gathered at the northern mountains:
En route they traverse this high gazebo,
Leaving behind a swath of piled mist.
If visitors here remain a long while.
Leaving, they'll find their robes and sleeves soaked through.

vi *The Altar of Illuminated Bamboo*[126]

Earth piled up was shaped into an altar,
Strategically positioned deep in the bamboo.
And therein lies a single "poet's rock,"
Where one can sit, hemmed round by the cold jade.
Don't say, few people know the spot:
In these realms, no vulgarity is allowed.

vii *The Hall of the Cassia Rock*

I have heard of Yangshuo Mountain,
Rising ten thousand feet above the ground!
This solitary peak stands in the courtyard here:
A fantastic rock,[127] that is quite like to it.
Loving it, I often come alone,
As many as three or four times a day!

viii *The Pavilion with Views in All Four Directions*

Peaks and ridges attached to Mount Liang,
Islands and sandspits following to the River Han:
The look of autumn tints these screen-like scenes,
Left and right for two hundred miles!
Such a landscape—who could describe it?
In lingering sundown clouds, alone, I lean on the railing.

---

126 This is a playful variation on Wang Wei's poem:

> I sit alone in the hidden bamboo grove,
> Playing my lute, and whistling mystically.
> Deep in the woods, no one knows I'm here,
> But the bright moon comes to keep me company.

127 Certain "fantastic rocks" were prized because of their resemblance to famous mountains.

ix *The Pathway Overhung with Vines*

Long vines clutching towering trees,
In darkness obscured by mist and fog.
"Already hanging a hundred feet or so,
Were you to grow still longer, just where do you think you'd go?
I'd appreciate it if you didn't grow any more:
You might hurt the one to whom you're attached."

x *The Embankment of Upward Swirling Clouds*

How many twists and turns up the layered battlements?
Every winding marked by patterned rocks.
Loving the place for such perfect beauty,
I never tire of coming, slow cane in hand, each evening.
The birds and creatures must think it strange,
Encountering this crazy man every single day!

xi *The Northern Studio*

The most awesome deities up in Heaven
All reside in places to the north!
Here is a studio that faces them directly,
And I fear it has been stricken with a demonic curse!
Whenever I pass by here, I *run*,
Not daring to rest a single instant!

xii *The Chess Studio*

They say the Northern Battlement is highest,
And up there stand the tallest trees.
Hanging vines form a tightly woven curtain,
And in the center has been built a little hut.
Here sometimes I invite guests from beyond the world of men,
To dissipate one hundred woes with a single game of chess.

xiii *Mountain Hall*

Why would they name a hall "Mountain?"
Layered rocks here form cliffs and scarps.
And I myself am basically a "cliff-cave" man:
Whenever I come here, I never want to leave.
The office clerks gorge me with vulgar documents,
So visiting this spot, I'm ashamed of my official cap.

xiv *The Serene Retreat*[128]

I know that Movement is an illusion,
And since I know it, already it's not Serenity.
So naming this retreat "Serene"—
Was this not to start a conflict in the self?
Let me say this to the man in the retreat:
Don't take Serenity to be a fault!

DYJ 14/8a-10b; no. 13 in Anthology, p. 139

169 *A Fantastically Shaped Pine Tree at the Guanyin Cloister*

Fantastic pines I've often seen,
    but never one like this;
Every time I come to visit,
    I mention it to the monks.
Should they encounter wind or thunder,
    it surely will protect them;
I'd only fear it might grow horns
    and fly off in the air!
Autumn sounds surround the hall,
    accompany fasting chimes;
Nighttime shadows invade corridors,
    and face the Buddha-lamps.
Wei Yan and Bi Hong[129] no longer in the world,
Should we wish someone to paint it,
    who could do so now?   *DYJ* 13/2b

---

128 The argument here, almost Chan (Zen) in its paradoxical nature, is expressed by someone, perhaps Wen Tong himself, aware of the dichotomy between Movement (or Action) and Serenity (or Inner Quietness), but who has continued living in the world of Action, or officialdom. Perhaps at times he has tried to convince himself that Serenity is an evasion of responsibility or duty—a classic argument against Buddhist monasticism, for example, since the Six Dynasties period. But his more spiritual side argues that one should pursue Serenity, as do Buddhists and other practitioners of reclusion. Poem 180 is another by this title.

129 Wei Yan and Bi Hong were eighth-century painters famed for their depictions of pine trees. Wen Tong, himself a master, of course, declines his own challenge.

170   *The Dragon Well at Northern Chan Temple*

> The divine dragon[130] north of the city
>   has been gone for many years;
> But recently, the people say,
>   he's returned to his old haunts.
> Deep, deep with the crystal pool,
>   all unapproachable,
> Even one hundred paces off
>   bones tingle and hairs rise!
> But this year at Xingyuan
>   seasonal rains have been delayed;
> Folks from there beseeched the dragon
>   for just a few sparse drops—
> A fragrant mist rose to the sky,
>   clouds burgeoned everywhere;
> All night long, a great downpour
>   spread hundreds of miles around.   *DYJ* 13/3a–b

---

130 A favorite subject for Wen is the role of dragon deities in controlling rainfall; these deities, however, are fickle, sometimes helping, as here, but sometimes not responding at all. Such cases may be interpreted as indications that the deity has moved quarters. The dragon deities, in addition, inspire awe if not fear, and their petitioners often evince feelings of trepidation in approaching them.

171   *Staying Overnight at the Palace-Shrine for Offerings to the True Ones*[131] *at Dipper Mountain*

The mountain is shaped like the Dipper,
    undulating forms,
Head-star pillowed, Handle-star to hold to,
    ten thousand fathoms high.
Modern people do not know
    the fire-dates up here;
But in the past, explorers found
    peaches of immortality.[132]
The moon's Divine Frog still hides out here,
    with congealed gemlike marrow;
The Spiritual Crane often returns,
    complete with feathers of jade.
All night long the pines and cedars
    sound with Heaven's voices:
Filling the sky, they must be playing
    the Immortals' cloudy gongs.
                        DYJ 13/4a–b

---

131 The True Ones would be apotheosized achievers of immortality. The terrain described is based on *fengshui* geomancy, with the mountains and the constellations in a corresponding relationship, and therefore a particularly numinous locale for the appearance of the magical fruits mentioned below.

132 "Fire-dates" and "peaches of immortality" are fruits eaten by Immortals, hidden only in certain sacred mountains. The idea that much of the lore known in the past has been forgotten today is consistent with the pre-modern view of a general degeneration of knowledge over the centuries, a striking contrast with the "progressivist" model of history of later periods.

172   *Great Snowfall at Mount Liang*

> A bitter wind blows howling on my house,
> Toward morning even fiercer than before.
> It must be coming from the top of North Mountain,
> All night long, spewing this ferocious snow.
> The recluse, forbidden to drink wine,
> His body as chilly as if wrapped in iron.
> All he can do, in these "dragon rags"[133] of his
> Is sadly chant poems, a sound that never ends.   *DYJ* 13/4b–5a

173–176   *A Temple at Zhongliang Mountain—*
            Four Quatrains

i

> Terraces and halls, veiled in darkness,
>   mountains towering high;
> Wisps of cloud reflecting light
>   in skies all vast and clear.
> Leaning forward, I gaze straight down,
>   sick of that dusty world—
> How could I grow a pair of wings,
>   fly up to the Ninefold Empyrean?

ii

> Misty ridges, multi-hued blue-green,
>   frosty woods all red;
> Storied towers, tiered pavilions
>   piercing fog and cloud.
> My heart is filled with lively spirit,
>   I just can't fall asleep;
> All night long, filling the mountain,
>   wind ringing wind-chimes.

---

133 "Dragon rags" refers (apparently ironically) to a rough blanket, like those used to cover oxen at night.

iii

Clustered peaks to south and north,
    competing in craggy splendor!
As if spilling waterfalls into great gullies,
    splashing with vast waves.
I love them so much, I want to bring them
    into the realm of a painting,
But no great masters alive today,
    how could this be done?[134]

iv

The ladder-like stone path to the abbot's quarters
    winds about the cliffs;
And who, on that remote summit
    added yet another hall?
It commands a view straight to the River Han,
    a hundred miles away,
A single stream like a thread,
    heading down to Yangzhou.   *DYJ* 13/6b–7a

---

134 As elsewhere, Wen, a master himself, declines to accept the challenge of capturing
the scene through painting.

177   *Beneath Clear Skies Climbing the Northern City Wall*

Rains accumulated, already more than a month,
Such a long time, preventing me from wandering here!
These cloud-girt mountains have troubled my dreams;
Now, weather happily turns clear and bright.
The places where I loved to come and go
Are now all covered by lichens and moss.
All along the moat, new flora abounds:
I don't know the names of more than half of them!   *DYJ* 14/5a

178   *At the Mountain Hall—Impromptu*

How many days with no official work?
In Mountain Hall, such pure inspiration!
Responding to poems—hard, with such a backlog!
Pills made from herbs—rush to make Pure-Bright.
Scraping off rocks—new angles now appear;
Irrigating vegetables—late shoots push up.[135]
All of this achieved in leisure from business:
Lowering my head, I laugh at dusty hat-strings!   *DYJ* 14/6a

---

135 The inner couplets describe "leisure" activities that have pressures of their own. There is a stack of poems accompanied by requests to "respond to" or "echo" them. Herbal medicines are best concocted in the spring; if delayed, the quality of the herbs might deteriorate. Caring for the rock garden also involves hard work. And yet the poet is still able to "laugh at dusty hatstrings," that is, to feel happy that he has escaped the drudgery of office.

179   *The Pavilion of Purity*

In the main office, very little commotion;
In study and pavilion, hardly any meetings at all.
Thus at leisure, I joy in mat and pillow;
Anxieties calmed, sick of documents . . .
A solitary flower brightens the deep copse;
Hidden chirpings are heard from thick leaves.
Here am I able to grasp the Principles of things:
A realm of Truth into which I can actually step![136]   *DYJ* 14/6a–b

---

136 The interesting final couplet implies that contemporary Neo-Confucian discussions of Principle (*li* 理) and Truth (*zhen* 真)—the two joined in modern Chinese as *zhenli*, truth,—have a tendency to sound abstract, whereas in the world as perceived from the Pavilion of Purity these "abstractions" take on concrete reality; one can even walk right amongst them! One is reminded, remotely, of Charles Williams' philosophical-supernatural novel, *The Place of the Lion* (1933), in which Platonic ideas actually appear to the senses of a cast of characters living in ordinary, contemporary England. But Williams goes much further than Wen in that all the "ordinary" animals, plants, etc., disappear as they are subsumed into the Ideal forms of which they were mere projections or manifestations.

The realm (*jing* 境) in the last line will also conjure up the phrase *jingjie*, 境界, another "realm" referring to the conjunction of external and internal worlds in human experience as evoked in literature, a usage today associated with the modern poet and thinker Wang Guowei (1877–1927), but anticipated in certain Ming dynasty critics, as I have previously argued in "The Panoply of Images: A Reconsideration of the Literary Theory of the Kung-an School" (Christian Murck and Susan Bush, eds., *Chinese Theories of the Arts*, Princeton University Press, 1982, *passim*). Here it appears that it is already being suggested by Wen Tong. Williams seems to tread related ground as well: "Foster . . . had made himself a place for the lion and it seemed the lion was taking possession of its habitation; its roar echoing in the wilderness and the dry places of the soul" (*The Place of the Lion*, p. 148). A perfect crossroads or even fusion between subject and object seems to be envisioned; we may also recall how in Su Shi's poem, Wen Tong "himself became bamboo."

180 *The Serene Retreat*[137]

I wonder, who was it who first built this place?
I admire you for your great diligence!
Nestled in a deep spot, among gigantic trees;
Fully shaded, covered by towering vines.
Seated here, just as quiet as the realm;
Not one person comes to irritate you!
The whole bed, covered with rough bedding:
Such is Maoguan,[138] basically living like a monk!   *DYJ*, 14/6b

181 *Beneath Clear Skies Strolling in the West Garden*

Driving rains, just now clearing up;
At tip of woods, brilliant evening clouds.
The pine pavilion from its cliff overlooks the panorama;
The bamboo path, slanting, enters sloping ground.
Flowers fall, preserved by the thick grasses;
A stream emerges, runs shallow along the sands.
Zhigui[139] is happy, even in poverty:
Hearing now a symphony performed by a pondful of frogs.

DYJ 14/7a

---

137 See poem xiv of the series 155–168 for another with this title.
138 Dao Gai (477–548), courtesy name Maoguan, though serving for much of his career as an official, lived a very frugal life and refused to surround himself with the trappings of high office. A friend, seeing his rough bedding, exclaimed that he was living just like a monk, and indeed Dao was very interested in Buddhism.
139 Kong Zhigui (448–501) was a noted nature poet. Wen Tong compares himself to Kong, or rather assimilates his identity.

182   *The Verandah of Golden Shadows*

> I open the verandah, gaze down at the pure stream,
> Right in the midst of a grove of tall bamboo.
> Those frosty trees embrace their icy knots;
> Brisk air gathers from all four directions.
> The master is sick of vulgar guests;
> Instead, daily he associates with This Gentleman.
> The moon now rises—cold shadows form,
> And my lapels flap with gemlike moon-dust.   *DYJ* 14/7a

183   *Suddenly Remembering the Tall Bamboo in my Old Garden, I Wrote this Poem*

> The tall bamboo in my hometown garden
>   turned with the eastern stream;
> Occupying the water, invading the sands,
>   ten thousand branches of them!
> I am traveling the official circuit,
>   no hope of retiring now;
> This Gentleman must be blaming me,
>   so slow to come back home.   *DYJ* 14/7b

184   *Sent to Inspector of Punishments, Jingru, at the Time Assigned to Wuxing*

> Railed cantilever roadways, deserted,
>   west of Wuxing . . .
> Yet the Inspector's entourage in raucous clatter
>   comes galloping with evening.
> You'd think it was a flying Immortal—
>   but surely, he will dismount?
> The magnificent scenery hereabouts
>   must enter his chanted poems!   *DYJ* 14/7b

185   *Zijun Makes an Excursion to Sand Stream Cave*

Hearing there is such a place as Sand Stream Cave,
His Excellency places chocks before the wheels
    of his official carriage.
And again, it seems one is exploring the Cave of Yu,
Or perhaps he is a man escaping from the evils of Qin!
Umbrella-shaped rocks are ancient in appearance;
Bejewled chambers are springlike in atmosphere:
"Should you meet someone riding in a cinnabar carriage,
Be sure to ask him for a tiger-stripe cap."[140]   *DYJ* 14/7b

186   *Requesting a Painting of Geese: Sent to Inspector Wu of Jingzhou*

Cold shadows in chaotic disarray—
    Qin Ridge moon;
Traveling late on the high road—
    clouds over dunes and mountains.
On your trip back, should you meet someone
    able to render geese,
On some future journey, let me accompany you,
    and beg a flock from him.   *DYJ* 14/8a

---

140 Since Sand Stream Cave is the sort of place where Immortals are likely to roam, the final couplet suggests that should you meet one, try to obtain from him the "tiger-stripe cap" emblematic of achievement in Daoism.

187 *Preparing to Travel to Yangzhou to Undertake a New Appointment I Write of my Old Place of Reclusion in East Valley*

Evening visitors? Not one comes,
So alone I walk into East Valley.
The garden there has already been completed:
The scenery is truly uncommon!
Nobly patterned, pines along the cliff;
Statuesque, bamboo beside the creek.
The bracing air touches sleeve and lapel,
All fresh, as if just newly washed.
A cold waterfall splashes against wild rocks,
Cleaning off the piled-high gemstone jades.
Drought-stricken streams now flush with overflowing wetness,
Ground covered by the verdancy of lichens, moss.
Rare birds serenely perch, leaning on each other,
Feathers brilliant and polychromatic!
Some fly high, now low, singing to each other,
But never flee, as if they were quite tame!
Mysterious flowers, mixing red and purple,
Raindrop-dotted, wildly fill my field of vision;
I sit here long, 'til a soft breeze comes,
And every so often, the scattered, lingering perfume . . .
This is the place where years ago I studied,
And just the same: the old thatched room!
Although it is a bit bedraggled,
Just a few wooden beams would fix it up just fine.
I open the door, wipe dust off studio windows,
Scaring up innumerable bats!
Every which way, spider webbing hangs,
No choice but to brush them down myself,
There, on the wall: faint characters,
Most of them once written by myself!
Those days, painstaking plans to make a living:
Oh, how grimly, bitterly I strove!

Now, thirty years have gone by,
And already the "lamb-ham's fully roasted!"[141]
Ever since I've entered the path of officialdom,
I seem to have stumbled with every step.
What I feared the most is files and documents;
What I yearned for was the simplest of vegetables!
But what outstanding luck!
I found myself drawing the Emperor's salary!
Unqualified, I found myself in the company of great scholars,
Hanging my head, often feeling inadequate.
Submitting repeated petitions to serve in the provinces,
And the posts I got were all out in the sticks!
Although it's true I was paid two thousand,
Could I dare deny my incompetence?
Then the court promulgated the "New Policies,"[142]
Trumpeting them as a blessing to the world!
Though I found them to be corrupted jokes,
The penalties they came with were quite severe.
How could anyone serving as an official at that time
Not enforce them urgently?
So I adopted the path of moderation,
Hoping thus to meet the enforcers' demands.
I have always hated treating people harshly:
How could I bear actually to punish them?
Not as though I didn't want to advance my career,
But—I truly feared being tortured in Hades!
Yesterday, I returned from the Han River region,
Here to pass the season of great heat.
With friends and relatives I would gather daily,
With them to enjoy *sincere* conversation!
Also, I wish to travel about with them,
Casting off my hat-pin, removing court robes!
To retire has been my plan for several years:

---

141 A "lamb-ham's fully roasted" is an expression of time swiftly passed.
142 The "New Policies" are those promulgated by Prime Minister (and superb poet) Wang Anshi; they found disfavor among most of the literati, who considered them to constitute a burden upon the people. His measures have been discussed and debated for centuries. See *Reform in Sung China: Wang An-shih (1021–1086) and His New Policies* by James T. C. Liu (Cambridge: Harvard University Press, 1959).

Just one summer and one winter simply not enough.
But now I must go off to Yangzhou,
There to be "nurtured," like chickens or geese!
Poverty being the norm for scholars,
Why should I let it press upon me?
If my "baskets and gourds" were all ready,
I could follow in the footsteps of a former worthy.
But alas! The mouths to feed are many:
I'm not like Yan Hui, all alone!
And, "In the east are over a thousand horsemen,"
Urging me on to leave this place at once!
So, on the long road once again,
Face wreathed in smiles, heart shrinking up inside!
How could Yuanming—hermit—be a vulgarian?
Fortunately, here are still pine trees, chrysanthemums.[143]

143–144

---

143 The closing fourteen lines of this poem, one of Wen's most ambitious and important, are a sustained inner dialogue, persuading himself that despite his long-standing yearning for retirement to a quiet life, he must after all feed his family. The "former worthy" of the ninth line from the end, named two lines later, is Yan Hui, the famed favorite disciple of Confucius. He was known for living content in poverty—satisfied with a single basket of food, and a single gourd of wine—but he, after all, was single and it was therefore relatively easy. But the poet still sees himself as on a par with Tao Yuanming (see note 40), who quit his official post to retire among his beloved pine trees and chrysanthemums. These poetic flora at least are awaiting Wen's ultimate exercise of the "retirement" option. In the sixth line from the end, he quotes from the anonymous poem "Moshang sang" ("Mulberries on the Paddy Paths"), usually considered to date from the Han dynasty. He is applying the imagery to the mounted escort he must travel with as an official.

188   *Mooring Late at Gold Ox*

My whole body feeling now
    the freshness of late frost;
Short reins dangling from the horse's head,
    I let him freely walk.
Setting sun now gathers in
    the shadows of sparse trees;
Brisk winds utterly cut off
    the sound of a waterfall.
I've gazed my fill of beauty spots—
    time after time, farewell!
I've inscribed new poems everywhere,
    each a real gem!
Yet, in the end, one must defer
    to Pan the Magistrate:[144]
So much natural talent displayed
    in his "Westward Journey" poem!   147

189   *Passing Blue Mud Ridge*

Iron Mountains in the first month,
    crisscrossed by snowy patches;
Wishing to find signs of the spring's east wind—
    to sky's edge none are seen.
But then, just as I pass Blue Mud,
    spring is doing well:
Along the streams, beneath the woods
    is seen the flowering plum!   148

---

144 Pan Yue (247–300) was famed both for his good looks and his poetic genius. His series of poems on the death of his wife is particularly outstanding. Here, however, Wen Tong feels that his own poems during this journey in the western regions (en route from Shaanxi to Sichuan) cannot compare with Pan's famous "Prose-poem on the Westward Journey."

190   *Along the Road to Datao, Seeing Chrysanthemums*

> Glorious flowers, cold-weather mums
>   braving the frost so fresh!
> Arrived to keep company here in the mountains—
>   all yellow—with regular plants.
> They don't strive to bloom at the height of spring
>   along with the other flowers,
> Simply content, in places remote,
>   to waft solitary perfume.
> All the others with their vulgar display
>   are not the authentic beauty;
> Only this subtle mist of theirs
>   counts as real fragrance.
> But then I think: Which "white-robed friend"
>   is here to bring me my wine?
> And thoughts go back to my hometown,
>   the hedge chock-full of happiness![145]   148–149

191   *At Changju*

> Mountain scenes fill the western tower:
> How many layers until the Yangtze's reached?
> Peaks and ridges—just like a Li Cheng![146]
> Streams and valleys—Fan Kuan alone could do them.
> At the furthest extreme: clear skies, mist hovering;
> In secluded depths: evening vapors congealing.
> There's just no way for me to paint such wonders;
> Already back down, now I climb back up again.   149

---

145 The last two lines, as expected, bring in Tao Qian (Tao Yuanming, see note 40), the poet par excellence of chrysanthemums, and references in his poetry to "gathering chrysanthemums at the eastern hedge," as well as a friend in a "white robe" who showed up with some wine just when he had run out.

146 Li Cheng (919–967) and Fan Kuan (fl. 990–1020), mentioned in the subsequent line, are two supreme masters of Chinese painting.

192   *From the Way-Station Tower at Changju*

> Bracing air floats through the void,
>   purple-blue-green thick:
> Across the river, without end,
>   truly remarkable peaks!
> If you, sir, wish to comprehend
>   the painting of Yingqiu,[147]
> Just take a look, there, in the east,
>   fifth layer from the ground.   150

193   *Sent to be Inscribed on the Bamboo Studio of Master Ze
of Kaiyuan Temple*

> Master Ze's been planting bamboo,
>   for thirty years so far,
> The bamboo grown, filling the courtyard,
>   breathing out green mist.
> These blue-green dragon-sons and grandsons
>   so flourishing and full,
> Their ancestry must be traced back
>   to Wei River valley.
> Absorbing wind and storing rain,
>   shading the walls of the hall,
> No one dares approach them lightly,
>   so cold and dignified!
> Their fragrance always enters in
>   among the Buddha-thrones;
> Their leaves fall, but don't reach as far
>   as *sutra*-window seats.
> They're pruned and trimmed, until they seem
>   as if they had been washed,
> Preventing wild branch-whips from
>   escaping beyond the railings.

---

147 Yingqiu is an alternate name of master painter Li Cheng, mentioned in the previous
poem and note.

Master Ze is lean and strong,
    just like an aged crane:
His tattered monk's robe droops several feet,
    exposing his left shoulder.
His hand counts rosary pearl-beads
    as he chants from Sanskrit books,
Statuesque, as if someone
    had molded or carved his image.
Morning, he strolls, dusk, circumambulates
    below the bamboo trees,
Unwilling to leave the courtyard
    even to beg for fasting alms!
Among the ancients, it's quite true,
    were lovers of bamboo,
But how could they compare with him,
    mind focused as his is!
But I, too, all my life have been
    fanatical like this,
And know a thing or two of how
    to depict them with brush and ink.
Encountering the Master, I can say,
    I've met a real soul-mate,
Except I regret I'm still held back
    by *karma* of this world.
When again will we face each other
    beneath a brilliant moon,
Sitting as long as the pure shadows last,
    discussing mysterious Zen?   151

194   *During a Heatwave Seeing a Sick Ox in the Fields*[148]

> Out in the fields a sick ox, how pitiable he is!
> Hide and hair all withered, horns drooping low.
> Nostrils agape, he can only pant with all his strength;
> Legs down to gaunt skeleton, as if there were no skin.
> The herdboy sits silently—
>   he's stopped trying to get him to move;
> The farmer stands hands folded—
>   he can only sigh.
> Driven by morning, worked by evening,
>   strength now given out:
> You may well die, and yet the master
>   will never even know.   29

195   *Living at My Country Home*

> Never again will I go to the city!
> Wild mountains cut this village off.
> Clouds and vapors supply my desk and mat;
> Streams and rocks assist wine-cup and zither.
> Sick so long my muscles have gone limp;
> Slept so much my head and eyes aswim.
> No one ever visits in this valley—
> Only moss climbs to my pine-tree gate.   8

---

148 Poems 194–196 appeared in the *G. W. Review,* Vol. 9, No. 2 (1989).

196   *On Wild Ducks*

Pair by pair your patterned wings
    touch the rippling stream;
How few are those who can achieve
    such innocence as yours!
Ten thousand acres of green waves
    supply your bill and craw;
Along a weir in chilly light
    you dry your feather robe.
As rain withdraws from each island now
    you murmur in quiet quacks;
As wind blows over the other shore
    you fly off with soft flaps.
Best to find a place out in the middle of the flow:
Be tranquil, and do not approach the wharf of fishermen.   154

197–226   *Miscellaneous Poems on the Gardens and Ponds of
Defense Residence—Thirty Poems*

i *Lake Bridge*

Flying bridge spanning Crosswise Lake:
Lying there, just like a giant rainbow.
I ask: "Within a single day,
How many people cross over you, back and forth?"

ii *Crosswise Lake*

Long lake, straight from east to west:
Rippling wavelets, guarding the inner chamber.
The panorama is of lotus blossoms:
Cloud-broidery from the Heavenly loom.

iii *The Library*

A pure stream winds around the courtyard,
Green bamboo sets off verandah railings.
If you sit here, what is there to do?
It's suitable only for carving printing blocks.

iv *The Pond Iced Over*

At sunset, the pond already frozen,
Fluttering, fluttering, down come ducks and drakes.
They have no fear of the coldness *in* the pond,
As they spend the night *on* the ice's surface.

v *Bamboo Embankment*

Patterned stones among the blue-green moss
Lead you in to the deep embankment.
Don't shake the green gemstone-like bamboo;
When least expected, dew will fall like rain.

vi *The Lotus Studio*

Morning sunlight beautifies autumn wavelets,
Lotus appearing beyond the deep bamboo.
Who opened this blue-green broidered screen
On limitless silver candles all alight?

vii *Rubus Rose Cave*

Soft stems adorned with heavy bloom,
Clustered on trellises, forming what seems a cave.
In this place, should you wish for fresh fragrance,
Rely on the wind to send some your way.

viii *The Valley of Magical Bamboo*[149]

A thousand carriages with kingfisher-feather canopies,
Ten thousand spear-stands,[150] propping spears sunk in verdancy.
It must have been the Immortal of Gepo Mooring[151] who
    planted them:
I wonder where he's hiding now?

ix *The Pathway of Golden Oranges*

The golden orange is surely a wondrous fruit,
Insufficiently prized by the locals.
I hear there aren't many in the upper garden:
Who is willing to transplant a few up there?

x *The Bay of Reeds*

Withered reeds, circled by frosty wind;
In evening cold, they rustle out loud.
Limitless numbers of little birds
Are grabbing places to stay overnight, as guests.

xi *Smartweed Islet*

A solitary islet, deep in pink smartweed,
Cold reflections bright in crystal waves.
At times, a pair of egrets visits here,
Flying in to beautify the scene.

---

149 See poem 253 for another with the same title.
150 The character qi 錡 usually refers to a stand for bows, but is used in conjunction with another word meaning a stand for weapons such as spears; I suspect the latter is what Wen Tong has in mind here.
151 The magician Fei Changfang is said to have thrown his walking stick into the water at Gepo Mooring, upon which it transformed into a dragon. The bamboo are compared with canopies, and then with weapons, which in turn may have evolved from the magician's staff turned dragon!

xii *The Kiosk for Viewing Clouds*

The Ba Mountains—*east* of the kiosk;
The Qin Range—*west* of the kiosk.
In the kiosk, if you roll up the blinds,
The place fills with monochrome cloud.

xiii *The Terrace for Awaiting the Moon*

At the wall's end, they've built a tiered terrace,
Reached by a hidden path that turns beneath the treetops.
Often here I wait for the brilliant moon
To climb, and climb, and reach the heart of Heaven.

xiv *The Gazebo of the Two Pleasures*[152]

Mount Zhong: who says it's "tranquil?"
The Han River: who says it's "active?"
These views derive from error:
Have you never applied "humaneness" and "wisdom?"

xv *The Terrace of the Heavenly Han River*[153]

On the northern shore, so many pavilions and halls!
The very first you climb is this terrace.
The terrace is so high, with its panorama of clustered peaks:
Over ten thousand miles of clouds jutting, towering.

---

152 This seemingly hermetic poem is a witty, Zhuangzi-like reversal of Confucian "common sense." According to the *Analects*, 6:21, as translated by James Legge, "The Master said, 'The wise find pleasure in water; the virtuous find pleasure in hills. The wise are active; the virtuous are tranquil . . . '" But from this kiosk, the mountains appear to be active, that is, in dynamic motion (as in Chinese landscape painting), while the Han River, from a great distance, actually seems to be "tranquil," that is, stable, not flowing. Zhuangzi might have included this poem in his chapter on the "Relativity of All Things." The implication of the last line might be that true humaneness and wisdom are flexible and open to different views of reality as shifting in different circumstances.

153 The name of the Terrace refers to the Milky Way. The name is particularly appropriate here because of the proximity of the earthly Han River.

xvi *The Pavilion of Clerkly Reclusion*[154]

The bamboo hedge is like a chicken roost;
The thatched hut resembles a snail shell.
At my tranquil desk, I'm quiet, as if in Zen meditation:
Completely unaware of folks who come and go.

xvii *The Pavilion of Bamboo in Frost*

The towering pavilion is in the deepest, hidden place,
Right in the center of the grove of tall bamboo.
Sitting here so long, cold starts to bother me:
I must think of standing, to take time out.

xviii *The Pavilion of Dang River Waterfall*

The source, a branch from Dang River,
Rolling, rolling, emerging below this pavilion.
How very deep must be Crosswise Lake!
Day and night, we see this water splashing in.

xix *The Pavilion of No Talking*[155]

Who set up a bench for loafers here?
Perfectly suited to my decrepit, lazy state!
Whenever there's the slightest break in public affairs,
I must come here, and sit, silently.

xx *The Pavilion of Dew-Fragrance*

Last night's dew covers the dawn flowers,
Such elegance!—a pure perfume wafts forth.
With each breeze it permeates my shirt, my sleeves,
With scent that will not dissipate for days.

---

154 The phrase "clerkly reclusion" is an apparent oxymoron that perfectly describes the subject of many of Wen Tong's poems: the poet holds office as a local magistrate, in a place so remote and tranquil that he might as well be in true reclusion.
155 A witty way of describing what actually is the opposite of "laziness," Chan (Zen) meditation!

xxi *The Pavilion Which Encompasses Void*[156]

Following stone steps back from circling the walls,
Entering bamboo, I see railings encompassing—void.
Gazing out, fine scenes are everywhere:
I'll lean on my stick, and just linger a while . . .

xxii *The Pavilion of River Radiance*

Crosswise Lake releases overflow waves,
Rushing, roaring, spilling with cold flow.
The sun's shadows climb higher in the woods,
Pure light-beams tremble on the windows here.

xxiii *The Pavilion that Spans the Stream*

A little bridge spans the crystal stream,
A pavilion on it, four pillars and a roof.
The place, remote, few people ever cross,
But—fluttering, fluttering—down come egrets, gulls.

xxiv *The Pavilion for Spring Purification Rites*[157]

A cascade imitating that "winding river;"
Here at the Spring Purification Festival
　　fine guests enjoyed themselves.
But the drinking's over, the scene ancient history,
When again will that Shanyin man appear?

---

156 In Buddhist thought, emptiness or void (Skt. *śūnyatā*) underpins everything, but the term is also used to indicate a subtler mode of Being.

157 A type of wit, in which a recent event is subsumed under a famed event of the past. The "Shanyin man," Wang Xizhi (303–361), most famous of calligraphers, once held a Spring Purification gathering at the Orchid Pavilion (Lanting), in the Shanyin area, beside a "winding river," and the prose preface he composed, along with the poems by the participants, became extremely famous, while the event itself became an iconic embodiment of literary gatherings. In this poem, the most likely interpretation is that Wen Tong and friends held such a gathering here on the third day of the third month, as was traditional (the so-called *shangsi*, 上巳, day), and in the poem, what we take as a description of this event is imperceptibly transposed into an allusion to the Wang Xizhi event seven centuries in the past. See poem 318.

xxv *The Southern Garden*

Farmers, mulberry gatherers with the break of day
Come rushing out, like the crazy flow of a blue-green river:
"Have the mulberry fruits ripened yet, or not?"
"Don't know! But we've heard the yellow warblers sing!"[158]

xxvi *The Northern Garden*

Spring wind—and quite a lot of it!—
Blows into this Governor's house.
I must share this joy with the people of the county:
Peach and plum blossoms filling the garden.

xxvii *The Harbor of Cold Reeds*

A lowering moon illumines the frozen lake;
How very brisk the air this dawn!
Both banks darkened by snow and mist:
Ducks and gulls fly off from the hidden harbor.

xxviii *The Huts of the Country Folk*

How isolated, the huts of the country folk,
Hedge-lined alleys dotted with brambles, reeds.
Every time I pass these humble gates,
Thoughts of retirement rise in my heart.

xxix *The Pavilion Decked in Blossoms Like Embroidery*

Profuse reds, stacked high unto the clouds,
Thickly clustered greens, in tiers like high waves.
Should the god of greenery come down in search of spring,
Filling the entire garden would be portable screens[159] for him.

---

158 The singing of the yellow warbler has been understood since ancient times to signal ripening of the mulberries. The silkworms dine on the leaves, but the state of the fruits may help determine the state of the leaves; also, medicinal properties are attributed to the former.

159 Portable screens were carried to shield kings or emperors from view. Here, the natural ones would be the stands of bamboo. See also poem viii of the series 37–46.

xxx *The Retreat of "This Gentleman"* [160]

Clumps of bamboo enwrap the circled eaves,
Their pure shadows blue-green like a river.
Whoever knows the feeling of love for This Gentleman
Once across the bridge, will always come here first.

DYJ 15/7a-10a; ten in *Anthology*, pp. 157–159

227 *Evening Snow on the Lake—Sent to Jingru*

Northern wind blows snow,
    covering Crosswise Lake;
All the birds are homing to perch,
    sun about to set.
I sit alone on the lake-view verandah,
    no one comes at all;
The woods look just as if
    you'd hung your *Painting of Birds at Night*. [161]   161

[*Poet's note*] This is a marvelous painting in Jingru's collection.

---

160 See no. 252 for another poem with this title. "This Gentleman" was the name given to bamboo by master calligrapher Wang Xizhi's son, Wang Huizhi (d. 388), himself an exemplary literatus and famed calligrapher. He loved bamboo so much that he planted nothing else; when someone asked him why, he answered, "How can I live a single day without This Gentleman?" The anecdote became so well-known that Japanese court-woman and diarist, Sei Shōnagon, in her *Pillow Book,* a masterpiece of Japanese literature, uses the allusion when a group of courtiers challenge her literary knowledge by silently holding before her a sprig of bamboo: "Oh, so it's This Gentleman!" Greatly impressed, the courtiers rush to inform the Emperor of her knowledge and wit.

161 Poem 153 is also about this painting, remarking on the occasion of Wen's friend, the collector, Zhang Jingru, showing it to him.

228–249   *Written at Leisure in the Water-View Hall of the
          Official Headquarters—in Six-Character Meter*[162]

i *On the Lake*

On the lake in pairs the birds are floating now—
Beside the bridge, fine willow branches hanging low;
Exactly noon, in the pavilion, nothing new:
The Governor[163] has come here just to chant his poems.

ii *Sitting Alone*

No announcements made of guests now at the door;
Already put in order, documents on my desk.
Sitting alone beside the water, beneath the woods,
It's just the same as my hometown, retired there.

iii *Lake Bridge*

Lake Bridge to the north hugs flower embankment;
To the west of Water-View, is Bamboo Village.
Raining, raining, through light fog beams reddish sun;
Vast, so vast, in delicate mist, a blue-green dusk.

iv *Playing my Zither*

Dot after dot, fresh duckweed adorns the water's surface;
Hazy, hazy, wild catkins twirl in wind.
All day long, playing the zither, sitting silent,
There is a man above the pond in the pavilion.

v *Tranquil Viewing*

Ten or more patterned fish play in the water;
A single pair of colorful ducks sleep on the sand.
Tranquil viewing—What I fear? To scare them off!
Not one word, I lean on the railing, sunset now.

---

162 There are 26 poems, four of which, xi through xiv, have been omitted here.
163 The Governor is Wen Tong himself.

vi *Pavilion Hall*

Pavilion Hall, in perfect peace, spending the day;
Garden woods, silent, silent, passing spring.
"Please screen in the bamboo shoots—I'll show the guests!
Don't sweep away the petals—that would be annoying."

vii *"Flowing Water"*

Four monks from Qin came by—a great discussion!
Just one Chu man's book—*Encountering Sorrow*.[164]
Done reading it, I think I'll play the "Flowing Water":
This is when the gentleman is happiest.

viii *Repaying the Country*

Repay the country? Don't forget to give your all;
Serve as official? No use in discussing "accomplishment."
Don't even ask about—*Ha! Ha!*—pursuit of pleasure;
No point in writing *Alas! Alas!*[165] on empty air.

ix *Hearing About the Dao*

I've heard about the Dao—I am no narrow pedant;
In reading books, though, willing to be quite old-fashioned.
My writing? I'm amazed I'm so against the times!
Though I love painting, who knows if I'll make "Divine?"[166]

---

164 It was the ancient poet of Chu, Qu Yuan, who wrote *Li sao* (*Encountering Sorrow*), a masterpiece of Chinese literature, on the occasion of his undeserved exile. "Flowing Water" is a staple of the zither (*qin*) repertoire.
165 This seems to be an elemental presentation of a philosophy more Stoic than Epicurean. It was Yin Hao, an exiled official (d. 356) who is said to have shown his unhappiness only by writing in the air the words *duoduo*, "Alas! Alas! [What a strange affair!]."
166 The Divine Class (*shenpin*) would be the highest level of accomplishment in painting or calligraphy.

x *Xiangru*[167]

What need was there for Sima Xiangru to call in sick?
And why did Tao Qian have to quit his official post?
Just humble yourself—whoever won't get on that way?
Acting "as if stupid" brings peace everywhere.

xv *Egrets*

Sheltering from rain, in bamboo here and there;
Taking the wind beneath the willows, fluttering.
Serenely huddling among cold smartweed—painting-like!
One stands alone on clear-sky sand—so lovable!

xvi *Lotus*

Greenish seeds now fill the receptacle, not full-grown;
When yellow silk surrounds the husk, that's when they'll bloom!
But, let me ask: Who is it they would urge to drink?
In formation now they dip their golden cups!

xvii *Gathering Lotus*

The guests, headcloths askew, walk out onto the bridge;
The girls, skirts splashed all wet, are out upon the lake.
The cassia sweeps and orchid oars—where are they now?
Lotus flowers, leaves of lotus—limitless.

xviii *Kingfisher*

When he sees a longish beak, he hides away;
If he spies a few slim fish, it's then he dives.
But let me warn him: "Don't come to the near-side shore!
There's someone there who'd love to grab your feathered robe!"[168]

---

167 Sima Xiangru (179–117 BC) was one of the great court poets of the Han dynasty. Late in life he became quite ill and turned down an official position on the plea of illness. We are also told that he often called in sick to avoid court duties. The image of a "sick Xiangru" is well established in literature, although usually with the implication that the illness was quite real. Wen's point seems to be that both Sima and Tao Qian, whose quitting of his position for a preferred life of quiet retirement is iconic, were "trying too hard," that the true Daoist way would be to accept circumstances and "go with the flow." The greatest wisdom seems like stupidity in Daoist thought—just as "[T]he wisdom of this world is foolishness with God" (1 Corinthians, 3:19)—and the "greatest skill seems like clumsiness," according to the *Dao de jing*.

168 Kingfisher feathers were prized for use in embroidery and jewelry.

xix *Red Hibiscus*[169]

While holding dew—that's when you boast of loveliness;
Wind-shaken, before you know it—petals fall!
The gentleman out on the lake now laughs at you:
Morning, blooming, evening, fallen—what's the use?

xx *Blue Stork*

I always hate the ducks when I'm in quietude;
But you, once full, do not disturb the fish and shrimp.
Your calm demeanor is just the way I'd like to be—
I ask you, sir: What sort of pleasure do you feel?

xxi *The Carriage Studio*

Where level lake is calmest, there's a red retreat,
And in the depths of weeping willows, painted bridge.
Desk-napping, fragrant mist and dew both moisten me,
Casting fishing line, my robe floats with the breeze.

xxii *Written Impromptu*

A calf goes rambling off to munch on sprouts—no problem;
A crow[170] alights to grab some meat—I look the other way.
Creatures require trust if they're to be moved by each other:
When things are tabooed in your heart, then there is trouble.

xxiii *The Northern Bank*

Winding gazebo, overlooking the reddish lotus reflections,
Round retreat building, centered in green bamboo shade.
Outside the gates, is there anyone who really can paint?
Let him come and make for us a folding screen of this scene.

---

169 The *zhujin*, or *Hibiscus rosa-sinensis* is the subject here. Most varieties of hibiscus do, in fact, have flowers that last only a day.

170 Crows are supposed to be emblems of bad luck. The idea seems to be that rather holding on to such taboos as this, we should allow all creatures to be themselves. "Trouble" here would be any sort of conflict or disharmony.

xxiv *Singing of Myself*

I sit in silence in the Pavilion for Viewing Paintings;
I walk a little along the Shore for Chanting Poems.
Folks call me "The Governor who Steals Leisure";
I call myself, "Mr. Salary-Robber."

xxv *Again Presented to the Egrets*

Your neck like a gemstone hook just slightly bent;
Your legs like tubes of jade, profoundly statuesque.
Here on the lake, the waterfowl are innumerable,
But who amongst them is as stylishly elegant as you?

xxvi *Written at Leisure*

Sent out into exile, for shame on Zipu![171]
Gone home to retire, how praise-worthy of Yuanming!
Let me just ask: How can the Recluse of Seven Pines
Possibly compare to the Gentleman of Five Willows?

DYJ, 16/5b-9b; eight in *Anthology*, pp. 162–163

---

171 Zipu or Zheng Xun (degree 828) was an official of the late Tang whose checkered career included exile, imposed upon him, whereas Yuanming (Tao Qian, see note 40) chose to leave officialdom. The former called himself Recluse of Seven Pines, while Tao wrote a brief autobiography of himself, one of the first in Chinese literature, referring to himself as Gentleman of the Five Willows, which he had planted in front of his house.

250   *Following the Rhymes of Zijun's*[172] *Poem, "Paintings of Snowy Mountains"*

First-class streams and first-class mountains,
    in six matched hanging scrolls!
All are full of snowy feeling,
    and true cloud-like appearance.
You, sir, surely will recall—
    beneath Flying Immortal Tower,
Right in front of Soaring Carriage Pavilion—
    the very same peaks as here.   pp. 164–165

---

172 Zijun is Xianyu Shen (1019–1087), a poet who composed thirty quatrains "echo-ing" those of Wen Tong on the gardens at Yangzhou (see above), as did Su Shi. (Four of these are given by Li E in *Songshi jishi*, Vol. 1, pp. 361–362.) And like Wen, he was recognized for his *Chu ci*-style poems (one is included in *Songshi jishi*). All three men were friends. Xianyu was also an *Yijing* (*Book of Changes*) scholar, as well as a courageous official who would speak his mind, as in his opposition to Wang Anshi's "New Policies." What is described here would appear to be a major work of art, no less than six hanging scrolls meant to be displayed side by side to constitute an enormous single composi-tion. Few such works survive today. For one, by the great early-Qing master Gong Xian (1620–1689) and consisting of four contiguous hanging scrolls (each measuring 280 x 58.1 cm, so that the whole composition would be over nine feet tall and over seven and a half feet wide), see Stephen Little *et al.*, *Seventeenth-Century Paintings from the Tsao Fam-ily Collection* (Los Angeles County Museum of Art and DelMonico Books-Prestel, 2016), Catalogue 70, pp. 414–415.

251   *Singing of Bamboo*

[*Poet's note*] This poem is formed of lines from one to ten characters in length.[173]

Bamboo!
Bamboo!
Sternly cold,
Freshly green.
Banks of Xiang River,
Bend of Wei Stream.
Curtain made of blue-green broidery,
Lances, spears of greenish jade.
Heart void, different from other flora,
Virtue-knots strong, beyond ordinary trees.
Branches turned to dragons, entering Immortal slopes;
Pitchpipes singing, summoning wind in divine valleys.
Moon goddess Chang E's scarf and skirt calmly fluttering,
Wind arising from this ocarina, pure susurrating tones.
In this grove drinking wine, fractured shadows trembling
     in the cup;
On these rocks playing chess, light umbrage shadowing
          the board.
When Qu Yuan the official was banished, he loved only
          sweet pepper
          and orchid;
When Tao Yuanming the gentleman retired, he sought out
          only pines
          and chrysanthemums.
If we admit that when it comes to a character of noble beauty,
          no one matches you,
Then when it's a question of painting your austerely elegant form,
          no one's more gifted than your humble servant!   165–166

---

173 Poems of this unique type were pioneered by Bai Juyi and his friends. For an example by Zhang Ji (ca. 766–ca. 830), see Jonathan Chaves, *Cloud Gate Song: The Verse of Tang Poet Zhang Ji* (Warren, CT: Floating World Editions, 2006), poem 6. The final lines disparage two luminaries of elegant taste, Qu Yuan and Tao Qian, for somehow failing to grasp the wonders of bamboo, which Wen boasts he himself is best skilled at capturing in art.

Bamboo and Rocks, Li Kan (1245–1320). Pair of hanging scrolls, ink and color on silk, each 74¾ x 21¾ in (189.9 x 55.2 cm). Metropolitan Museum of Art, image courtesy of the C. C. Wang Family, Gift of The Dillon Fund, 1973.

252   *The Retreat of "This Gentleman"*[174]

Mottled, mottled, dropping sheaths
    exposing the new bamboo,
The radiance of white powder scintillates,
    the fragrance forms a mist.
I always love This Gentleman,
    and sit here silently,
So much better than looking at
    millions of mediocre men.   167

253   *The Valley of Magical Bamboo*[175]

The pond sends a stream into the valley,
    wavelets rippling, rippling,
Bamboo joins both shores together,
    mist so thick and full.
In search of hidden mystery, I head straight in,
    as the scene grows ever wilder,
And before I know it, I no longer seem
    to inhabit the world of dust . . .   167

---

174 See poem xxx in the series 197–226 for another with the same title.
175 See poem viii of the series 197–226 for another with the same title.

254–266   *Miscellaneous Poems on the Serene Residence of Li Jianfu—Thirteen Poems with Preface*

[*Poet's preface*] Jianfu, being invited to serve in the Palace of Great Peace, had a group of pavilions and other structures built, expanding on a residence in Chang'an neighborhood [of the capital, Bianjing, modern Kaifeng?]. Here he spent his leisure time in various enjoyments. Thus he has written thirteen poems about the place, and sent them to me from far away, asking that I do the same. Loving the pure, remote feeling they convey, I put together some verses to append after those he composed, but feeling ashamed that they are not of excellent craftsmanship, I do so merely for the purpose of meeting his request.

i *The Serene Residence*[176]

What action suits a time of purity?
Retire! And sing the ode on "Building a Retreat!"
Recently, I hear, at your new residence
One does not seem to be in the capital!

ii *The Serene Old Man*

Declining nasty busywork of "Rice" and "Salt,"[177]
You get the noble task of helping in palace and shrine.
You claim for your own the joys of a leisurely position:
Why ever let any vulgar folks know?

---

176 Line two refers to a poem In the classic *Shijing* (*Book of Songs*) entitled "*Kaopan*" 考槃, the term used by Wen Tong, and generally interpreted as meaning "to build a retreat." The irony is, that when the government is "pure," that is, well-ordered and humane, there is no need to serve, so one might as well retire! By this interpretation, the Confucian view of good governance is not that far removed from the Daoist one of *wu-wei,* or "doing nothing."

177 From ancient times, salt, iron, and other commodities were regulated if not monopolized by the government; elaborate bureaucracies dealt with them.

iii *The House for Playing the Zither*

How are you to express your mysterious feelings?
You've got the sounds of this ancient *wutong* wood![178]
Let me ask: When you get to a point where you're playing
    really well,
Who is there to come and listen to "The Walk of the Crab"?

iv *The House for Playing Weiqi Chess*

Totally at leisure—what can you do now?
Only *this* will while away days and nights.
Wrapped up in contesting the board with a guest,
Would you hear the man who just stopped knocking at the door?

v *The Calligraphy Studio*

Fine silks spread on the table frame,
And limitless, the wondrous calligraphy!
I imagine, that to sit there in that setting
Would be to feel just like an otter "sacrificing fish."[179]

vi *The Painting Studio*

If we try to rate the paintings in this studio,
None is of the second rank!
Staunch rocks and wild bamboo:
These two should be hung in the chief place of all!

[*Poet's note*] These two paintings are the work of my own brush, and so
I touch on them in jest.

vii *The Springtime Verandah*

Sunbeams brighten the vast expanse,
Heaven's breath warms the atmosphere.
Flora, trees, surround the courtyard railings:
Fresh perfumes are inhaled morning, noon, and night.

---

178 *Wutong* was the favored wood for making zithers, or *guqin*. "The Walk of the Crab"
is the name of a zither piece, imitating the crosswise walking motion of the crustacean.
179 As James Legge long ago noted, the otter's habit of leaving over a portion of its prey
led to the folk-belief that it was offering a sacrifice in thanksgiving for his meal. Here the
idea may be that there would be a religious feeling in such an ambience.

viii *The Autumn Verandah*

Fresh gusts bring sighing, soughing movement:
Blue-green tree-shade, all susurrating softly.
But most of all I love when the moon comes at night,
And window-silk is filled with so many cold shadows.

ix *The Bamboo Verandah*

As iron, as stone, the branches are strong;
Iced-over, frosted, the knots are round.
Quietly swaying them, the wind blows long and low,
Serenely glowing on them, the moon is lovely, lovely.

x *The Juniper Verandah*

Blue-green feathers, clustered how tightly;
Sapphire balls,[180] arranged so thickly.
Who suspects that both the trees and the man
Are grandsons of the Heaven of Supreme Purity?

xi *The Water-View Pavilion*

The cold current daily ripples here,
Winding, turning before the low balustrade;
I wonder, when the bright moon beams down its reflection
Who comes to play with it in the rushing stream?

xii *The Retreat for Retirement*

Before you've grown old, you've requested to retire;
You titled this place yourself, inscribed the words.
You've so much talent, you soon should be promoted;
But then, would you be able to keep this name?

xiii *The Northern Hall*

Serene Residence completely finished,
On remaining ground you built this new hall.
No point in planting the lily "Forgetting Sorrow";[181]
You have no sorrows that you need to forget!

DYJ 17/9a–10b; no. 9 in *Anthology*, p. 168

---

180 The "sapphire balls" would be the berries of the juniper.
181 The day-lily (*Hemerocallis flava*) is invested with rich meaning in China. One alternate name for it is *wangyou*, or "forgetting sorrow."

267 *The Bird of One Hundred Tongues*[182]

The myriad feathered creatures jump on spring—
  that's when their throats and beaks come alive!
Filling the woods, unlimited are their calls
  beneath the clearing skies.
In the southern garden, just when flowers and trees
  are flourishing at their height,
The little, tiny ones, the large, imposing ones—
  all of them come to sing!
Hidden on branches, adorning leaves—
  does anyone *make* them do it?
They're unwilling to stop for a moment,
  but just keep jabbering away!
Amongst their number, the Hundred-Tongue
  is the most nonsensical:
His mouth is filled with the cries of other birds
  which he's learned by heart!
He has not a single word to say
  that is his very own.
All he does is squawk and screech
  as freely as he pleases.
Morning after morning, he perches upon
  my tall willow trees,
Screams bursting through my single window,
  where lingering moonlight gleams.
This recluse is sleeping deeply,
  a sweet, delightful snooze,
But has no way—what can he do?—
  to deal with this alarm!
Who's that kid who always carries
  his slingshot around with him?
How can I entice him to do me a favor,
  and come at crack of dawn?   170

---

182 The title refers to the blackbird (*wudong*), or *Turdus merula*.

268   *Asking Jingxun to Lend Me Mei Shengyu's*[183]
       Poetry Scrolls

    The other day I was reading your poems,
    And they quickened my anxious, sickening body.
    It was like sitting in wilting heat,
    And sipping ambrosia from a jeweled cup!
    The diction, solemn, the meaning fresh and striking:
    I daresay no other poet has written such things.
    And yet you did not pride yourself,
    But instead attributed all to your reverence for Shengyu!
    You recited several of his choice verses for me,
    And indeed, he seemed to be of the ilk of Meng and Jia.[184]
    Then you told me that you owned a family treasure,
    Two scrolls the size and heft of pillars!
    I have only now become enamored of this study,
    But always feel as if I've lost a sense of direction.
    I would be so happy if you'd loan these to me for a bit:
    Perhaps they'll lead me on the straight and narrow path.   177

---

183 Mei Shengyu refers to Mei Yaochen (1002–1060), a key figure in early Song poetry.
184 "Meng and Jia" would be Meng Jiao and Jia Dao of the Tang dynasty, also important poets, although opinions on Meng's poetry in particular were divided. No less a figure than Su Shi famously wrote in the opening line of a poem, "I hate Meng Jiao's poetry!" Wen Tong almost seems to be damning Mei with faint praise by comparing him with these figures; however, perhaps because his host admires Mei so much, he makes the gesture of wishing to borrow what appears to have been a complete edition of Mei's writings in the form of two huge scrolls. Wen's desire to flatter is also apparent in the extravagant praise he heaps upon his host's poetry. Today, "Jingxun" (or Jing Xun, if Jing is the surname as is possible) cannot be fully identified. We know he was a very close friend of Wen Tong, but little beyond this. For more on Mei Yaochen, see Jonathan Chaves, *Mei Yao-ch'en and the Development of Early Sung Poetry* (New York and London: Columbia University Press, 1976).

269   *Plucking Willow Branches*[185]

> Weeping willows, overhanging one hundred feet
>   of watery pond-surface;
> Wind settled, mist thick,
>   they're too weak to sway and curl.
> I'd pluck some long branches,
>   and send them to you on your distant journey,
> Except I fear that by the time they reach you,
>   they will have withered completely away.   180

270   *With "Yearn-to-Return" Birds on All Sides,*
       Written on the Spot

> In this gorge are plenty of crying birds,
> Cacophonous, impossible to understand.
> But of those who say, "Yearn-to-Return—"[186]
> The males sing it out, the females respond!
> In the gulley ahead, clouds are arising;
> From the mountains behind, the moon has already descended.
> Travelers are afraid to hear you, birds—
> With every note, another heart will break!   182

271   *On First Entering the Path along Two-Mile Creek*

> Tree colors crisscrossing mountain colors,
> Cicada tones mixing with creek tones;
> The traveler's feelings here, not jaded at all
> As he lets his horse pick its way through these scenes.   183

---

185 Plucking willow branches as a farewell gift is a long-established custom. On this oc-
casion, it appears as if the poet's friend is already a long way off, and any such gift would
have to be sent far away. This poem is repeated immediately after the series of twenty
entitled, "From the Repository of Painting," possibly implying that it too describes a
painting. See poems 301–320.
186 The cuckoo is the bird in question, whose cry is supposed to sound like *sigui* 思歸,
or "yearn-to-return," that is, to retire and return to one's native soil.

272   *The View from the High Terrace*[187]

View from High Terrace,
Gazing toward hometown,
A thousand miles away,
One corner of the sky.
Beyond vision's reach,
Vast expanse of void.
A single cloud flies,
It can't take me along.
How can I grow wings and soar
    out there to the southwest?

273   *Ballad of Suffering from the Cold*[188]

I ascend Taihang Mountains, ah! so tall and towering!
Sun about to set, ah! year draws to a close.
Entering the valley mouth, ah! emerging at the edge of woods,
Wind blowing so chillingly, ah! blowing my very bones cold.
Ice and frost congealed, ah! on jade peaks jutting up,
Sunlight shining above, ah! the sky seems all dried out.
In profusion, wilting and drooping, ah! flora and trees wither.
Pitch black, frigid, ah! mist and cloud darken fully;
Servants' feet all chapped, ah! horses' hooves wearing down,
A look at tonight's quarters, ah! simply breaks my heart!
Purse soon will be empty, ah! clothing all unlined,
Alas, these roads, ah! How punishing they are!   184

---

187 This is a *yuefu,* or "Music Bureau" title, dating in title and form from the Han Dynasty. The unusual meter is 3-3-3-3-3-3-3-3-7 characters per line. The poet adapts the ancient form to his present experience. His hometown is indeed far off to the southwest, in Sichuan.
188 Here is another *yuefu* title, in this case associated with one of Wen Tong's favored *Chu ci* meters, his mastery of which, as noted in the Introduction, was praised by Su Shi. In this variation, the exclamatory *xi* (兮, here rendered "ah!") occupies the fourth position in a seven-character line, dividing it into two three-character groups.

274   *Taking Off for Sickness on the Wutong Verandah*

Towering *wutong* cover me with new leafage;
They suffuse the courtyard with flourishing life.
How long the day seems to be,
Calmly the pure shade naturally shifts place.
In warmth, the inchworms hang down to the ground;
Beneath clear skies, birds sing all day long.
My sick elbows lean on the desk of withered wood:
Trance-like, I forget whatever worried me.   *DYJ* 15/5a

275–279   *Birds on the Lake: In All Cases Using Their Popular Names as Titles—Five Poems*

i River-Scourer [pelican]

The schools of fish see newly cleared skies:
Their ten thousand fins play in the clear freshness!
Suddenly, a pelican swoops down—
Startled, they dash back under the ice.

ii *Seven-Count Wags* [yellow wagtail] [189]

Fluttering, fluttering this precious bird,
Golden feathers glowing in cold sunlight:
He lands on the ice along the stream,
Sees someone, to a "seven-count wags" his tail!

iii *Trailing-White-Silk* [Asian paradise flycatcher]

On a flat rock I sit, deep in the woods,
Not wanting anyone to be able to find me.
On the stream's other shore, who is plucking strings?
—Several notes of the trailing-white-silk bird.

---

189 Also called the citrine wagtail. The website birdnet.cn cites an explanation from Sichuan gazetteers for its curious folk-name: In the Five Dynasties period (906–960) a monk asked Chan Master Honggao the meaning of this bird's name. Honggao responded, "Before you can count the full number of fingers on your hands, there will be no trace of him on the ground," that is, it will fly away before one can count to seven. A Zen Master might well concern himself with such matters because of the Buddhist doctrine of the illusoriness of phenomena, which are ultimately impossible to grasp.

iv *Slippery-Slippery-Mud* [bamboo partridge] [190]

Springtime, and Clear-Bright is here:
Filling the garden, flowers bloom in profusion.
I urge you, you "bamboo grove chicken":
Please, do *not* sing "slippery-slippery-mud!"

v *Grab-a-Jug* [pelican] [191]

The flowers have opened, already can be plucked;
The wine is ready, just the time to buy some!
This mountain bird understands what I want,
And urges me to "grab-a-jug!"   *DYJ* 15/10a–b

280   *The Kingfisher* [192]

At crack of dawn, there is a precious bird,
Fluttering, fluttering, landing on the fishing weir.
His body would hardly fill your grasp,
His feathers are clean and lustrous.
Some angel stitched blue-green mists
And made for him the robe he wears.
Scintillating, dazzling to my eye,
Not ordinary blue or yellow of this world!
Loving him, I sit here very long,
Fearing with a blink of the eye, he'd fly away.
Suddenly—a plunge into the clear ripples:
He's snatched some tidbit the size of a needle-point;
He does the same again, some three times, or four,
Then, satiated, he's full right to the throat!

---

190 The folk name derives from the sound of the bird's call, *ni-hua-hua*. The poet is afraid that rainfall would be conjured up by this call, and would damage the flowers.

191 As with the bird in poem iv, this name derives from the sound of its call, considered to be *ti hulu* or *hulu ti*. It seems odd to have two poems out of five referring to the same bird. Some pelicans do, in fact, perch during breeding season in the woods some distance from water, and perhaps in mountains. Or Wen Tong may have had in mind two different birds for poems i and v; however, the two names today are considered synonymous, and refer to the pelican.

192 Following well-established tradition, Wen Tong presents realistic descriptions of the kingfisher and other birds, while using them allegorically to send a warning to officials of high moral principles to be careful about associating with the unscrupulous.

Replete and satisfied,
He takes wing, returning to his old pond,
Flying, calling to his beloved mate,
And her cry is heard, harmonizing chime-like with his.
Meanwhile, ducks and geese
Are randomly scattered about the islets,
Stomachs glutted with a brew of noxious filth,
All over the ground, sunning themselves in brilliant light.
But most disgusting and evil of all, the *bald crane*,
Huge maw, legs endlessly long,
Stepping into the stream to catch water-snakes,
Gulping them down, along with globs of mud!
"I fear that when they see you, sir,
They'll wound you with a single snap:
In their hearts, how could they stand seeing
Your body all adorned with lovely patterns?
I urge you, sir, be careful where you perch:
The good and the ugly can't share the same land!
In this pure stream are plenty of fresh delicacies,
Sufficing to fill your stomach.
But the rivers and lakes are deep and broad:
What you'll 'catch' out there cannot be foreseen."   *DYJ* 16/2a

281   *This Joy*

Clerks dismissed, documents all filed:
This office seems like a mountain retreat;
So I go home, change to rustic clothes,
Take my stick and—where do I go now?
The garden pavilion is extremely refreshing,
Heavily shaded beneath tall bamboo.
Brushing off a rock I sit there all day,
Lingering on and on, not aware the night has fallen . . .
Then the mountain moon beams on me, all bright,
The forest breeze blows on me, all pure.
I chant out loud some ancient texts,
Strolling to and fro beside the pond.
Dew falls, and I feel the subtle chill;
To the southern window I return, head on pillow.
My heart serene, my soul naturally at peace,
Until the dawn I enjoy sweet, tranquil sleep.

The Envoi

"You lazy magistrate! What do you think you're doing,
Day after day, making this your routine?"
"All I'll say is—that's the way I am:
How can you possibly understand this joy?"   *DYJ* 17/3a–b

282   *Don't Sweep Away the Petals!*

Don't sweep away the petals!
Let them lie there, blanketing the ground!
So they pile up into mounds—what harm in that?
Just leave them! And it suits the mood of the Lord of the East!
Sir, do you not see:
    Yesterday morning the branches were fully blossoming,
Today in the courtyard, already withering?
In their lives, how long can they flourish?
And may I use this example to invite you
    to examine the Principles of Things:
First thriving, then fading—and both of these are Void!
And if indeed they are not real,
    it's basically all one!
All's to do is face the falling petals,
    wine filling your cup,
Every year, the same as now,
    let the spring wind[193] do what it always does.   *DYJ* 17/4a

---

193 The spring wind, under the command of the Lord of the East, always blows down the petals from the flowering trees beloved of the Chinese poets. The poet expresses an interesting combination of the current Neo-Confucian (or Lixue, "School of Principle") concept that there is a substratum of *li,* or Principle, underlying every living or non-living thing, and every process of nature, with the Buddhist concept that all is void, or illusory, lacking actual reality.

283   *The Water Mill*

Where water rushes, they made a water mill,
    the people of Jialing;
Canal-walls tall, bottom deep,
    grueling is the labor!
Within a radius of three and a third miles
    everyone shares this mill:
Wheat in, flour out, so nobody will do without.
But the workers here live in dangerous spots,
    what they can produce is meager;
For generations they've fed the folks
    who live along the river.
Oh, may the Court see fit to send an investigator,[194]
    to improve this use of water-power:
Please have pity on these straight-wheeled
    and slant-wheeled carts!   *DYJ* 17/6a

284   *The Bridge of the Heavenly Han River [Milky Way]*

Wind sweeps along both banks,
    the reeds have all dried out;
Sunlight sprinkles the whole land-spit,
    the ducks and drakes are cold.
Deep in the night, a frosty moon
    illuminates the lake:
This is when you *must* go out on this bridge,
    and lean on the patterned railing.   *DYJ* 17/7b

---

194 The poet's brief is apparently for easing the lives of the laborers who are tasked with maintaining this heavily utilized facility in an area difficult of access, as well as carting in and out the wheat and flour on dangerous slopes, where they must live as well to maintain the schedule of the work. If an Imperial inspector or investigator reports truthfully on the situation, perhaps something might be done to alleviate their situation.

285   *The Tower for Gazing at Clouds*

The southern peak, the northern ridge—
    from far, seem piled in layers;
Morning clouds and evening rain—
    so thick, like rising steam!
The tower is high—one hundred feet—
    the view, ten thousand miles!
Do you need some special reason
    to come and climb up here?   *DYJ* 17/7b

286 *An Inscription of the State of Jin*

In Chang'an, a dealer in epigraphic texts
Sold me an inscription from an ancient *ding*[195] vessel.
Nothing is known of its provenance;
No one has ever seen the like.
There are 119 characters in all,
Truly weird, tracing the shapes of things.
And the placement and arrangement of dots and strokes
Unlike our ordinary *zi* or *ding*.[196]
After consulting all the sources,
Its origin remains obscure.
The *Stone Drum Texts* of King Xuan
Have energy-resonance and fluent style;
Qin's first emperor's *Stele of Mount Yi*
Shows such high-stepping structure!
But I suspect that when the spirits wept
It was precisely because of the divinity of this work!
How can I get a deity who will never die
To carry it off to consult Lord Dating?[197]
Perhaps he'll be able to translate the text for me:
Reciting it will startle the world's ears!   *DYJ* 18/1a

---

195 The feudal state of Jin (eleventh century–376 BC) was located in the north Yellow
River Valley, modern Shanxi Province, and flourished as a producer of bronze ritual ves-
sels primarily in the seventh to sixth centuries BC. Wen Tong probably purchased a rub-
bing of the inscription on one of the *ding*-type vessels, tripods or four-legged square ones,
for the serving of sacrificial meats. Wen's words of praise throughout refer to the archaic
calligraphy that was revered both for its historical and aesthetic value, even though in
Wen's day such inscriptions often could not be fully deciphered.

196 Two of the simplest Chinese characters, *zi* 子 and *ding* 丁, are given as examples to
indicate the profundity of the gap between the ancient "seal" and other archaic scripts,
and their contemporary forms.

197 Wen hopes that he will be able to have the writing translated (or transcribed) by
Lord Dating, one of the legendary rulers of high antiquity, who presumably would be
able to read them. Wen also cites two of the most famous examples of ancient writing,
the *Stone Drum Texts*, which he attributes to the reign of King Xuan of Zhou (r. 827–782
BC, although most authorities today would place them in the fifth century BC); and
the *Stele of Mount Yi*, erected by Qin Shi Huangdi, China's first emperor (r. 221–210
BC), but with calligraphy by his Prime Minister, Li Si. The Stone Drums were famously
re-discovered and praised in a magnificent poem by Han Yu (768–824), in which he first
attributes them to King Xuan. But Wen claims the calligraphy on his rubbing is even
better, causing spirits to weep because man has robbed them of creative power, a conceit
often applied to great art or literature.

287   *A Proclamation of the Qin Dynasty*[198]

Where mountain currents wash the remote Ruan state,
A bronze object with seal characters emitted its ancient glow.
When I arrived to take office in Fengtian,
An old man sold it to me for just a hundred cash.
Reading it, it turned out to be by Qin's second emperor,
An engraved proclamation from the first year of his reign.
What it said was, "Laws, weights and measures:
These all were created by the first emperor.
But inscriptions only say, 'emperor';
After a long time, who will comprehend?"
And so he issues instruction to Li Si and Feng Quji,
Laying out all the details to the right.
The text is crisp and simple,
The calligraphy strokes are wonderfully fine.

But, Hai![199] What kind of man were you,
To dare to become a joke for ten thousand generations?
What you did was simply not right!
This might serve as a mere spirit-tablet.
So petty-minded, calling for eulogies of what is trivial!
Looking back, it's all lamentable!

---

198 The proclamation is generally known as *Zhao Li Si Feng Quji* (詔李斯馮去疾), or "Proclamation to Li Si and Feng Quji," written in 209 BC (the first year of the second emperor's reign). Wen's mixed feelings about this object are understandable. On the one hand, the text is well-composed, and the calligraphy is elegant, as it often is on relics of the Qin dynasty. But he despises the dynasty itself, as did all Confucian scholars, and especially the second Qin emperor, whose reign lasted only a few short years before the dynasty was overthrown in 206 BC and the mighty Han dynasty founded. The text of the proclamation is preserved, and Wen faithfully reproduces part of it. The rest consists of instructions to Prime Minister Li Si, and another official named Feng Quji, for correcting the inscriptions on legal documents, weights and measures to reflect the fact they were the creation of the second emperor's father, the first emperor and founder of the dynasty. Wen thinks it ridiculous that this short-lived dynasty should be eulogized in this grandiose manner. All the object was good for when made was to be a "spirit tablet" for the second emperor's father, to be placed in his ancestral temple, thus merely an object of self-glorification.

199 "Hai" is the personal name of the second emperor, Hu Hai, for whom Wen shows his low regard by addressing so familiarly.

Our local troops, already glutted with treasures,
Got hold of this, only to cast it off again.
It went flowing off, and landed in barren earth,
For a thousand years to suffer obscurity.
And so I realize, within this cosmos,
Some things are simply unpredictable:
Today, what is this object good for?
It just makes the observer laugh!   *DYJ* 18/1a–b

288   *Staying Overnight at Cloud-Screen Mountain Temple*

A blue-green ridge surges to the edge of clouds,
Precipitous, running and then again twisting.
A visitor enters this realm from the dusty world;
A monk is seen, as if standing in a painting.
The moon rises, a thousand peaks turn blue;
Wind starts gusting, ten thousand trees are cold.
Tomorrow, crack of dawn, I regret having to leave—
Let me at least lean once more upon the railing . . . *DYJ* 18/11a

289   *Listening to a Recluse from Mount Tiantai Play the Qin*

This recluse has mastered the essentials of the zither:
Who was his master? His master was Nature!
And since he says, "'Autumn Thoughts' is fine!"
We hear the roundness of his night-plucked tones.
Our ears are carried beyond lascivious bawling,
Hearts trembling before the fall of silence again.
But sir, please stop before playing the "Guangling Piece":[200]
One should not loosely sound the sad note of *shang*.

                                                      DYJ 18/11b

---

200 The "Guangling Piece" was famed for having been played by poet and zither (*qin*)
master Xi [or Ji] Kang (223–262) just prior to his execution for a political crime. It fea-
tures the *shang*, or sad "autumnal," tone from the pentatonic scale, and evokes the suicide
of a righteous assassin, who kills himself to assert the purity of his motive. Listening to a
recluse from the "Heavenly Terrace" (Tiantai) play his zither, Wen fears he cannot bear
the sadness of hearing this piece.

290   *Setting Forth at Night through Sanguan Pass*

> Wind blowing at the mouth of the ancient pass,
> Ten thousand trees explode, as if splitting.
> Freezing cold, a traveler from another land
> Mounts his horse in moonlight filling the pass.
> On plank roads frost shines brilliantly;
> Beneath stone bridges the stream is gurgling on.
> But, how unexpected!—In the dawn chill, even colder,
> Still, I can't help loving the snow on the mountain top!
>
> *DYJ* 18/12a

291   *A Game of Go²⁰¹ on the Northern Verandah of White Crane Monastery*

> Jetavana hides in this corner of the city;
> Here they've opened a verandah, remote, mysterious in feeling.
> The sun's shadows shift, but never reach here;
> The place always has the feeling of autumn.
> This is where I pass the time of scorching heat,
> A single game-board, and I forget the ten thousand affairs!
> Hustling and bustling, you folks outside these gates:
> Who among you comprehends the meaning found here?
>
> *DYJ* 18/13a

---

201 More popularly known by its Japanese name, *go*, the Chinese board game *weiqi* has been mentioned in works dating to the fourth century BC. Jetavana was one of the first monasteries founded for the Buddha.

292-311[202]

i Revenue Officer Song Fugu's[203] "Snowscape with Clear Skies along an Evening Stream"

Clearing weather transforms the clouded woods;
Cold radiance mixes with misted waters.
Those distant mountains: Where, exactly, are they?
So hazy, one can only point the general direction.

ii Early Autumn: A Landscape Stone-Screen[204]

Evening mists cut off the distant peaks;
Autumn's visage extends into the level forest.
A square of silk, merely one foot by one,
And yet these peaks and valleys seem so very deep.

iii Large Crabs by Intendant Kou Junyu

Crabs, by their nature, very hard to paint!
Their life lies in their pincers, and their legs.
But this man captures them most wondrously:
It seems their crabby motion can't be stopped!

iv Small Crabs

Carapace and shell and all those joints!
Connections rendered clearly with great craft.
Although you have so many limbs and legs,
You're able to move just like one single "coin."

---

202 These twenty poems occur in chapter 19 of *DYJ* under the heading *Huachu zayong* (畫厨雜詠), or "Miscellaneous Poems from the Repository of Painting." There is also a twenty-first poem which may or may not be from a painting (and has already occurred earlier in the collection as poem 269).

203 Song Fugu mentioned in poem i is Song Di (*jinshi* degree, 1023–1032), praised by Su Shi as the first painter to execute the fabled *Eight Views of the Xiao and Xiang Rivers*, which would become so important as a theme in later Chinese and Japanese art.

204 The term "stone-screen" usually refers to patterned rock-surfaces that seem to show natural landscape markings, mounted in wooden frames for a scholar's desk. But here Wen seems to intend a square painting on silk, possible used as a screen to guard or show to best advantage an inkstone.

v *Magpie Chicks by Huang Quan*[205]

Short feathers, already showing fluffy,
Weak pinions now just starting to jut forth:
But where has mommy gone off to now?
Mouths open, you're all stretching up for food!

vi *Hibiscus by Teng Changyou*[206]

A pair of stalks producing blossoms in the cold:
Each standing there as if with patterned feathers!
If we were to classify the masters,
You'd surely be in the top two or three!

vii *Fighting Oxen by Old Mao*

Oxen! Oxen! What're you fighting for?
Right here, engaging in angry battle!
The village herdboy must exercise his whip,
The farmer's wife comes running with fiery flare!
Eight or nine baby badgers,
Frightened, stand there, staring all around.
When will you disengage your horns,
Return to the thatched stall for the river-village evening?

viii *Ancient Trees and Cold Oxen by Deng Yin*[207]

A hoary cliff, angular protrusions,
    wild flora thriving everywhere;
A great tree, half dead now,
    giving rise only to withered mist.
The skinny ox, late in the day,
    is munching on mere grass;
Some boys, out in the cold weather,
    keep up their "coin-toss" game.

---

205 Huang Quan (903–965) is regarded as one of the first and finest bird-and-flower painters. His name becomes iconic in later centuries for the very best of this type of art, although authentic works by him are very rare today.
206 Teng Changyou, like Huang Quan, was a tenth-century master known particularly for his flower paintings.
207 Deng Yin is recorded in several texts as a master painter of Buddhist images, deities, landscapes, and bird-and-flower works.

ix *Cold Forest by Xu Daoning*[208]

Mr. Xu may have emulated Li Yingqiu,
But his ink-path, freely wandering,
    emerges from himself!
Intersecting branches, light and agile,
    like Pei Min's "Dance of the Sword!"
Wild vines, so fluent, free,
    like Zhang Xiao's calligraphy.

x *Marmoset Hugging an Oak Tree by Yi Yuanji*[209]

An ancient oak—hugged as if by a protrusion:
Golden marmoset, standing there, with freely flowing hair.
That year, along the road to Longshan Mountain:
I seemed to see this very scene,
    against abrupt layers of cliffs.

xi *A Doe Leading her Fawn*[210]

A tawny doe leads her tannish fawn:
Ears perked up—what has startled her?
On a high plain, imagine newly cleared skies,
Her hoof-prints are visible among the paddocks.

---

208 Xu Daoning (ca. 970–1051/53) is today recognized as one of the great Northern Song masters. Wen clearly spots the genius of this older contemporary of his, saying that even though he worked in the manner of the great Li Cheng (Yingqiu), he developed his own style. This is high praise indeed. The second couplet concentrates on the brilliance of his brushwork, always a prime concern in Chinese connoisseurship. The painter's brushwork is ultimately seen as deriving from calligraphic strokes. Pei Min's sword dance, especially the movement of his sword tip in the air, like that of a calligrapher's brush, could inspire artists. Zhang Xiao was presumably a famed calligrapher, like Pei Min, of the Tang dynasty.

209 For Wen Tong and the great painter of gibbons and other creatures, Yi Yuanji, see Robert Van Gulik, *The Gibbon in China: An Essay in Chinese Animal* Lore (Leiden: E.J. Brill, 1967), pp. 77–79, where he cites but does not translate this poem.

210 Yi Yuanji was also known for paintings of deer.

xii *An Egret in the Cold Among Withered Lotus and Broken Reeds by Cui Bai*[211]

Sparse reeds aging in a downpour,
Chaotic lotus withering beyond the frost;
But the one with most feeling is the white bird,
Here standing companion to desolation.

xiii *Pratyeka Buddha by Sun Taigu*[212]

Purisadammasarathi brings sacred fire
    producing correct thoughts;
Mahāsattva offers incense
    giving rise to the mind of faith.
The meaning of these two sages
    lies beyond brushwork:
Ah, that Taigu! How utterly profound
    the feeling in his work!

xiv *Thunder Capturing the Dragon*[213] *by Xu Zhongzheng*

Why, oh why has that dragon
    been exiled by Heaven above?
Because he wouldn't follow Heaven's command
    to bring fructifying rain.
Thus Heaven commissioned the Thunder Duke
    to seek him everywhere;
But where had the dragon hidden himself?
    Now, suddenly, he's caught!
He's grabbed ahold of, filling the sky,
    like a skein of silk dragged along;

---

211 Cui Bai (1004–88) was a bird and animal painter known precisely for scenes of the type described in this poem.

212 Sun Taigu was a well-attested painter of Buddhist subjects. The Sanskrit names of the two Buddhist sages depicted in the painting seen by Wen can be taken as generic descriptions of two types of "Pratyeka Buddha," that is, Buddhas who attain enlightenment individually, for themselves alone. For this term, as well as the Sanskrit names in the first two lines, Wen employs the Chinese transliterations; here as elsewhere he employs abbreviated forms to fit the requirements of Chinese prosody.

213 This most unusual take on the dragon theme is consistent with Wen's particular interest in the dragon as rain god, who here is deserving of punishment for failing to perform his duties.

Hailstone winds and fiery lightning
    curl and shoot each other.
The Thunder Duke spreads his enormous wings,
    and simply flaps and flaps;
He pulls the dragon, head and tail,
    nearly ripping him in two.
The dragon's strength, of course, no match
    for the Thunder's power!
The Thunder grows still more furious,
    the dragon loses heart;
One moment later, we'll surely see
    liver and stomach split!
The power of a thousand, the spirit of ten thousand,
    in just a few brushstrokes!
This master, and this work must rank
    as of the Divine Class.

xv *A Solitary Peak in the Snow by Fan Kuan*[214]

A great snowfall sprinkles the arc of the sky;
A solitary peak pierces the edge of the clouds.
Who is that man in the fishing boat,
Huddling in coarse woolens, facing the towering slopes?

xvi *Misty Waves Late in Autumn*

Straight on to ten feet of silk
He has depicted in full a thousand-mile scene.
The clouds and mountains, vast and deep,
    have already turned to autumn;
The misty waters, reaching far,
    have just entered a darkening realm
You, sir, must have acquired this painting
    not realizing what it was:
As for me, I lack the words
    to describe it adequately.

---

214 Fan Kuan (ca. 960–ca. 1030) is another supreme master of Chinese painting, whose masterpiece, *Traveling Among Mountains and Streams,* is in the Palace Museum, Taiwan. There, too, man's smallness in proportion to the vast sweep of nature is emphasized.

xvii *Spring Mountains*

On ridge and plain, plants and trees all flourish;
On stream, in valley, clouds and haze attract.
Who today transmits your brushwork?
Still the only one who grasps how to exhale harmony.

xviii *Autumn Mountains*

A solitary peak exposes hoary bones;
Sparse trees surge forth—their powerful trunks.
In the high hall, hung on a barren wall,
Breathing out fresh air continually.

xix *A Little Picture of Playing the Deerskin Drum by Liang Xin*

Tall *wutong* trees interspersed with weeping willows,
A jade mansion filled with mysterious purity.
The "Third Lad" sits center-hall,
Flanked by beauties to left and right.
On altar cloth, incense is offered,
Crouching beasts spit out the blue-green flame.
A bejeweled table holds the sounding-box;[215]
In dazzling confusion, colored sleeves whirl and intersect.
A tattooed slave flips back both cuffs,
Bows and stands, ready to display his skill.
The lord looks at him, with a smile,
And the whole chamber is filled with harmonious energy.
Who would have thought a single foot of silk
Could depict so fully the feeling of being in Heaven?
How must those who *heard* this have felt?
Even just *seeing* it dispels "mustiness."

[*Poet's note*] Emperor Minghuang once said that a tattooed barbarian playing the deerskin drum "can dispel the mustiness of the zither."

---

215 The "sounding-box," or *kong* 椌, was a percussion instrument consisting of a wooden box, open on top, and a stick which was inserted and rattled around the inside of the box to produce a percussive sound.

xx *Zhong Kui by Mr. Pu*[216]

A freezing wind howls fiercely,
  and the moon turns bitter, sad;
The owl flies, the fox howls out loud,
  pervading cemetery tombs.
Clumps of thorns, wild, scattered stones
  are cloaked by country fog;
The ancient shrine is stripped and barren,
  choked with fallen, withered trees.
Below, there are three ghosts in view,
  whistling as they gather together:
Whose home will they visit first,
  to infect them with the plague?
Pain and fever, swelling, itching—
  quick to spit these forth!
Blocking up the breathing tube,
  distending people's stomachs.
Call the shaman! Summon shamaness!
  Chant exorcistic prayers!
Old men frightened, old women rushing
  to set out ritual implements!
The "thatched tray," the "boat of grass"
  will open the Five Highways: [217]
Bowls of rice, skewered meats
  in wild disorder offered.
The demons grab the offerings,
  and carry them away;
Here they sit bolt upright,
  and they suck and guzzle them.
But all of a sudden—they see something
  that frightens them to death!

---

216 Zhong Kui is the Demon Queller, the exorcist par excellence. For an excellent study
of this theme in painting, see Stephen Little, "The Demon Queller and the Art of Qiu
Ying (Ch'iu Ying)," (*Artibus Asiae*, Vol. 46, No. 1/2, 1985, pp. 5–128). This article in-
cludes a translation of the current poem (pp. 27–28).
217 The "thatched tray" and "boat of grass" are implements from Chinese folk religion.
Sometimes made of paper, they are burned so that they will travel as offerings to the
spirits or ancestors. The Five Highways are the five cardinal directions, the four compass
points and the center, from which deities may be enticed to bring prosperity.

A god, so dignified! comes riding in
    upon a gigantic bull!
Shouting in front, protecting from behind,
    two boys are put to work:
This god *eats* ghosts for breakfast,
    for lunch and dinner too!
But his stomach is still hungry now,
    his expression angry, fierce!
The ghosts from far take just one look,
    are totally dismayed!
Dashing here and there to hide away,
    no time to warn the others!
Their wine is spilled, meat falls to the ground,
    mixed with the mud and dirt,
Their souls and spirits fly away,
    their bodies bite the dust!
One of them enters among the trees,
    grabs hold with all four limbs;
One still tightly clutching his wine cup,
    glances, terrified, around.
Another hides himself away,
    turns back, spies angrily;
But the god forcefully catches him,
    and ties him firmly up:
While still alive, popped into the god's mouth,
    before ten steps are taken!
But though he bites and chews, it seems
    he's already had his fill.

Mr. Pu! How is it that
    you happened upon such a scene?
You've painted it, filling up the scroll,
    without a single error!
The brushwork and inkwork capture the ugly weirdness,
    so very terrifying!
And what has moved you to give it to me like this?
Waving away money with a gesture,
    unwilling to take a cent?

In days ahead, those asking for poems
    will surely be numerous:
And that's why I've tried describing it,
    laying out the entire story.   *DYJ* 19/1a–4a

312 *Prose-poem on The Terrace of Transcendence*[218]

It was just the time of abundance, spring's second month, ah!
I viewed the glorious richness of flora and trees.
Yet how much anxiety in my heart, ah!
Discouraged that I was alone, with no one to rely upon.
I climbed the surging watch-tower to gaze at the panorama, ah!
Hills and slopes ranging so high in zigzag patterns.
Exhausting the range of vision to the utmost distance, ah!
I could see only the brilliant shining of the floating beams
    of light.
Suddenly, there arose a whirlwind darkening everything, ah!
Scattering dark vapors to veil all four directions,
Thwarting my sense of direction, ah!
Confusing me entirely: Where should I turn now?
Sloughing off body, soul galloping so far, ah!
I set my course through the vast void, hurrying upwards.
Piercing darkness, I entered upon great expanses, ah!
Waving rainbow banners, and shaking flags of cloud!
Guided by long comets, I soared through space, ah!
Following the serpentine curves of rainbow-dragons.
Trailing colored ornaments to lead red phoenixes, ah!
Riding bejeweled carriage, urging on the blue-green krakens.
Crossing vast waters, emerging, sinking again, ah!
Traversing the Great Brightness, eclipsing its light!
Soaring ten thousand miles in just one instant, ah!
I leaned down toward the Nine Continents and viewed them all.

---

218 The poem is in a *Chu ci* meter, like all of those in the first chapter and several in the second of Wen's collected writings, *DYS*. Su Zhe, Su Shi's younger brother, and Zhang Lei, one of Su Shi's disciples, also wrote *fu,* or "prose-poems," about this spot, and Su Shi himself has a prose account about it. It was Su Shi who, in 1075, constructed or renovated the Terrace, in Shandong Province. The man who proves to be a guru to Wen Tong in this work may well be intended as a complimentary portrait of Su Shi.

And there was a person, so very fine, ah!
Alone in the eastern quadrant.
So many days had I been away, yet I could not forget him, ah!
Upright and pure, ah!
Upstanding, dignified.
He was clothed in Loyalty, Trustworthiness, ah!
And wore Literature as a robe.
Dazzling white within, ah!
All gem-like without.
Of orchid were his lapels, ah!
Of cassia was his robe.
Majestic, as if planted in place, ah!
He displayed official tablet.
He gathered all luminance to himself, ah!
Embodied perfect fragrance.
Any hagglng for worldly employment he has put aside, ah!
He roams beyond the world, letting himself go in complete
    freedom!
Wanting to follow him, ah!
I watched him from far away.
We circled "Ram's Horn," ah!
Made our way toward "Dragon's Throat."
Then we swerved to Yuyi, ah!
Trod upon the Fusang Tree.
Leaning next upon Mount Tai, ah! [219]
We lingered there a while,
Then descended to Transcendence Terrace, ah!
Where I bowed down beside the man.
"I have questions I wish to put to you, ah!
And this meeting is so rare!"
Without so much as a nod of the head, ah!
He told me everything in detail.
He made it possible for me to escape the net of the chaotic
    world, ah!

---

219 Yuyi is the region from which the sun rises in the morning, ascending from the
Fusang Mulberry Tree of the distant east. Mount Tai is the easternmost of the Five Sacred
Mountains.

And to undo the fetters that impede all things.
And with this, liberated, ah!
I emerged from the field of burdens,
Once again, as if a very Immortal, ah!
To return to my hometown.   *DYJ* 1a–2a

313   *The Pavilion for Appreciating the Harvest at Qiongzhou—With Preface*[220]

[*Poet's preface*] The Pavilion for Appreciating the Harvest was built and named by Magistrate Dou. For the sake of tracing the scene and depicting the meaning, various sage poets have inscribed their poems on plaques, and I myself contributed clerk-style script on a large scale. But it is according to reason that there ought to be a narrative about how the place came about as well, and I therefore also wrote this poem of one-hundred-fifty characters, like dust in the midst of so many gems! But the reason the grammar is so plain and the diction of the verses is so unrefined is that I wish the farmers and the wives who feed the farmers out in the fields and along the irrigation ditches to be able to understand them easily upon their being read out loud, and to memorize them easily for recitation, so that they themselves may use them to sing the praises of the Magistrate's virtue. In a word, I wish them to be easily used to teach. Thus I do not fear others' pointing out this poem for mockery, and I presume herewith to present it.

Peoples' reason for constructing a pavilion
Is generally some personal benefit.
So how is it that our Excellency
Has built one for an entirely different cause?
To the northeast of Linqiong
In clear order grow all the various crops.
The citizens love to apply their strength to them,
And not a year goes by without abundant harvest.
His Excellency therefore climbed the city wall,
And felt great admiration for these "many crops."[221]

---

220 This and the following six poems are from the Addenda (Add.) of the *DYJ*.
221 "Many crops" is a phrase from the ancient *Shijing* poem, "Datian" ("Great Fields").

Thus he proclaimed, "These fine grains
Are truly the realm of these my people!
If they always continue such application,
How could they fail to love this, their native soil?
And I, acting as shepherd to these folks,
How could I ever need to fear they might abscond?"
So he planned to build a structure here,
Visible to all, facing everywhere.
And he inscribed it with two words: "Appreciate" the "Harvest";
With meaning not limited to "build this and maintain."
And always would he command his official staff,
In a timely manner to make offerings of music,
Nobly to discourse of omens from On High,
Ceaselessly, never slacking off;
With libations of wine to venerate the great fields;
Pointing to them, he was greatly pleased by everything.
The farmers all say to each other:
"Who could ever claim that we are lowly?
The Magistrate indeed acts on our behalf:
And today as well he gives us a great feast!"

DYJ, Add. *shang*/1a–b

314 *The Hall of Three Self-Examinations*[222] *in the Subprefect's Office of Qiongzhou*

If you wish to speak of governing men
You must first start from *correcting your own self.*
When your self is corrected, the people will naturally
    be governed:
This charismatic transformation will proceed as if divine.
All the innumerable books of the sages
Make this point especially over and over again.
And later sages have held to this as a principle,
Never daring to backslide in forgetfulness.
And wishing to record this even further,
They even inscribed it on various objects:
Sometimes they'd illuminate desks, or walking sticks,
Sometimes they'd lay it out on dishes and bowls,
Or they'd inscribe it on official chairs,
Or even embroider it on girdles.
This is because those who walk the Way, though poor,
Would want this principle beside them day and night.
And after they'd been immersed in it for a long time,
Their supreme virtue would gleam, all brilliantly.

Luhou is a man of Suzhou,
Who wears righteousness as belt-ornament,
    and robes himself in humaneness.
He arrived riding in an assistant's carriage,
Teeth and hair those of a younger man.
When he opens his mouth to discuss government affairs,
Every issue is presented in perfect order.
In spring, the dew, in autumn, frost:

---

222 In *Analects* 1:4 Master Zeng said, "I daily examine myself in three ways: In my consultations with others, have I not been loyal? In my interactions with my friends have I not been trustworthy? Have I not actually practiced what I have received [from my teachers]?" The ideas underlying the name of the hall, and the poem, are from the *Daxue*, *The Great Learning*, attributed to Zengzi, Confucius's senior disciple, and quoted in the *Analects* passage cited. His utterances and writings were taken to be almost as authoritative as those of Confucius himself and are addressed primarily to those in positions of authority.

Awe to his clerks, love shown to his people.
And still he fears there might be some flaw in him,
Preventing the purity of his character.
And so alongside the office,
He built a study, to meet the year *jiayin* [1074].
This he inscribed, "Hall of Three Self-Examinations,"
A large structure with brand-new name-plaque.
The land is old, with a rural feel,
Streams and bamboos purify robe and headcloth.
His Excellency, when leisure allows, always comes in here,
Totally quiet, as if hidden completely away.
Entering deep into his mind, contemplating self,
He probes what is external, and further seeks within.
As soon as he sees anything inadequate,
He patches and repairs it, leaving not one iota of dust.
And then he will go ahead, and compose poems,
With perfect balance of diction and principle,
In due course, showing clearly cautionary lessons,
Wishing all customs to be pure.
Should he find any foolishness weighing him down,
He will bow again and again, not refusing many repetitions.
And if he humbles himself like this,
Imagine how wise the neighbors of this true gentleman!
I wish for the foundation of this structure
Never to encounter weeds and brambles:
If anything is broken, please, restore it,
So that this name is never obliterated.   *DYJ* Add. *shang*/1b–2b

---

The poem is also a reminder that meditative practices in China are not limited to Buddhism and Daoism, but are found in Confucianism as well. Also intimated is the idea that the self-cultivated leader emits a moral charisma which will affect those around him, to the point of encompassing the entire body politic.

315   *Inscribed on the Cliff on the Back Slope of Phoenix Mountain*

This view is uniquely beautiful!
Halfway up the sky—a zigzag railing appears.
Dust from Sichuan peters out right before my eyes;
Snow from barbarian lands fills my robe with chill.
Below the stream, the sound of rain is urgent;
On top of the cliff, the clouds have a dried-out look.
Groom! Don't tell me it's late and we should return:
I want to stay, to linger here a while.   *DYJ* Add. *shang*/3a

316   *Echoing Chen Jizai's Poem, "A Great Rainfall"*

Deeply black, the clouds seem on the boil,
Gushing hard, rain seems spilled out.
Suddenly flipped over, muddying the Silver Han;
Evenly wiped clean, purifying the Jade Rope.[223]
Thunder, so angry! Seems it will never end;
Wind, so bold! Blocking all other sounds.
Here, high in the tower, it's the start of the dog days,
And yet I'd still say my clothing is too light.   *DYJ* Add. *shang*/4b

---

223 The Silver Han refers to the Milky Way; the Jade Rope is a constellation.

317 *Presented to the Daoist Li Zhongxiang*

Already many years since I last saw you, sir;
My thoughts of you were limited to reading your fine writings.
Since I have come to govern this county,
    among deserted mountains,
I've had the pleasure of your name announced
    before the patterned spears.
Clapping your hands, energetically discoursing,
    still sparkling with energy!
The bold life-spirit that fills your heart
    yet radiates around.
Recently, I hear, you've purchased
    a pond with wild geese: [224]
Here, in the world of men, you are
    an Immortal walking earth.   *DYJ* Add. *shang*/5a

318 *Presented to the Gentleman of the Orchid Stream*

[*Poet's note*] Huang Sen, courtesy name Junqiao, a man of Yizheng.

Master Huang of Nanji—
All life long, his attitude austere.
From of old, he's been addicted to chanting poems;
Lately, his calligraphy has turned wild and crazy.
But alas, he ages among deserted mountains;
He must be recorded for future generations!
"At Orchid Stream, will you have the Spring Purification?
I yearn for you to continue what was done in the
    Yonghe years!" [225]   *DYJ* Add. *shang*/5b

---

224 Perhaps like the great calligrapher Wang Xizhi (see next), the recipient intends to receive inspiration for his calligraphy by observing the movements of the geese.
225 The Yonghe period (345–356) of the final couplet refers to the time that the great calligrapher Wang Xizhi and his friends held a spring purification ceremony at Orchid Pavilion (Lanting), probably the most famous literary gathering in history. See poem xxiv in the series 197–226.

319   *An Excursion to the Cloister for Leisurely Residence*

Time off from work, I visit "Leisurely Residence":
Hiking, viewing—what I just have to do!
But first, quickly, buy some wine at Dragon Mouth!
Too lazy to strike the wooden fish[226] in front of Buddha.

                                          DYJ Add. *shang*/5b

320–322   *Invocations Querying the God, with Preface*

[*Poet's preface*] In the fifth month, summer, of the year *bingshen* [1056], there was a great drought in Nanbin. The local people rushed *en masse* to the Quintessential Proclamation Pond to obtain divine water. As soon as they got some, they returned to their local shrines, there to pray for rain. And yet after more than ten days, there was no response. The people became terrified. The grain-crops withered away completely, and with nothing to eat, the people faced death. And they wondered, why did the god not prove his efficacy immediately, as he did in the past? All mouths opened in wails and sighs, and hearing them, I wrote these "Invocations Querying the God," and had them performed as songs. There are three of them in all, as below.

i

Upon the occurrence of this year's drought,
We called on all the spirits, but they were silent.
Calluses like molted silkworms, foreheads streaming sweat,
The people passed to distant regions, Yea!
Those whose gods had blessed them with moisture.
Carrying pots and jars, taking what extra drops they could, Yea!
Bringing them home in protected carriages.
They hoped for officials to pray truly, sincerely, Yea!
For some slight compassion on the people's starvation;
Shamans sang, shamanesses danced, Yea!
    Tongues flapping, wrists drooping down.
In the plains they cried out, in the fields called, Yea!
    Old men running, crones rushing too.

226 The "wooden fish" is a fish-shaped wooden block, struck to signal services and meals in Buddhist monasteries.

They wrote out fresh vows of purity,
　　spread them through their homes, Yea!
Presenting them repeatedly every day, with ever greater urgency.
I would like to query the god, Yea!
Have you no pity? Just what is it you're doing?

ii

The circle of the Ning Mountains, Yea!
　　the bays of Ning River:
Here hath our god resided, Yea!
　　for hundreds and thousands of years.
He hath been revered by local people,
　　as if he were a *deva*,
And at each drought, they got rain, Yea!
　　as easy as the flip of a hand!
Moisture emerged, irrigation flowed, Yea!
Yin-force behind, hot, dry air was gone.
Within the realms of Qin, Yea! for whole years, no barren earth.
But this Summer, the parched thirst of the fields, Yea!
　　Wind withering, and sun scorching!
I would like to query the god, Yea!
Why not get to work, and lay on a bit of rain?

iii

The god in the past, for his merit, Yea!
　　received of Heaven blessings.
He was robed in garments flowery, sparkling, Yea!
Capped in a crown of pearls and jade.
He resided in towered chambers, winding in and around, Yea!
Corridors and passageways connecting.
Brilliant, scintillating, dazzling, Yea!
　　twisting about mountains,
　　　　joining valley to valley.
And beneath those curtains, Yea! clouds stored with rain!
Sufficient to moisturize, Yea! all our Hundred Grains!
Why, then, so miserly,
　　unleashing the cruelty of the Drought Demon?
I would like to query the god, Yea!
And bring favor in place of this cruel insult.　　　*DYJ* 1/4b-5b

Opposite: *New Bamboo,* Gu An (ca. 1289–after 1365), Hanging scroll, ink on paper, 35¾ x 13 in (91 x 33.1 cm), 14th century. Palace Museum, Beijing.

THE PROSE OF
WEN TONG

1   *Inscribed after the Sutra of the Eight Teachers*[227]

Buddhist books carry accounts of Hell, stating that those who commit evil *karma* in the human world will upon death enter this realm and, depending on the comparative seriousness of their offense, will receive torturous punishment, without the slightest mistake. They depict in full the ways in which the punishment is administered, describing all kinds of bizarre measures. At first, I thought that these were simply incredible; but frequently they would be brought forth to admonish and influence worldly manners, and this produced results. My friend, Lü Jinshu, Editor of the Imperial Library, has described *The Sutra of the Eight Teachers*, narrating the events that occurred to the Chen clan in full detail, and in confidence has told me of his own personal experiences with these matters. Jinshu is by nature stolidly upright and rational. His statements are never fallacious. I subsequently acquired a copy of this text, and took it home with me to Sichuan, where I hoped to have it printed, so as to promulgate it. My idea was that should there be in the world anyone acting perversely and violently, devoted to a life of illicit action, although such a man might congratulate himself on avoiding official punishments of the Dynasty, and thus living until he dies avoiding a catastrophe from Heaven and keeping his hide whole, this text would indeed make him aware that within the Abysm of Hades the ordinances are bitterly cruel, and there is no way he can hope to be whitewashed, and thus get to escape! And so by means of fear perhaps it would be possible to change his heart and reform his actions, undergoing personal contrition and confession. For this *sutra,* should today's men convert through it, will establish great examples of brilliant results. The Śūraṅgama Man of the Way, Master Jishu,[228] is one who is expert at converting men. People have great faith in him. Perhaps he can take command of this task and commit some of it to this *sutra.*   *DYJ* 21/4a–b

---

227 The Eight Teachers of the title refer to killing, stealing, committing sexual offenses, lying, drinking intoxicants, sickness, old age, and death. What events befell the Chen clan are unknown to us today. Lü Jinshu, also Lü Xiaqing (1015/18–1070), was indeed one of the editors of the *New History of the Tang Dynasty*, coordinated by Ouyang Xiu. He has a poem and some further information in *Songshi jishi* (Vol. 1, p. 397). Like Ouyang he gathered epigraphic inscriptions and published them, and authored various other writings as well. Ouyang Xiu has a poem seeing him off.
228 For Master Jishu, see also *DYJ,* 21/5b-6a *zan.*

2   *Memorial Text on the Jiao Sacrificial Ceremony at the Palace-Shrine of Sheer Divinity*

On such-and-such a day of a month of a certain year, I, of the cohort of officials, on this very day, commission certain officials to offer incense, libations of wine, and sacrificial meats, thus to carry out the pure Jiao ceremony to the Great Sage, the True Primal Lord of the Golden Tower.[229] I am in humble receipt of the Letter of Pardon of the twenty-first day of the tenth month sent to all sacrificers, in which His Imperial Majesty, because the star-patterns have manifested admonitory warning, has universally pardoned every imprisoned criminal throughout the world. For let us consider that within the cosmos, should anything not retain its established position, the wrongful indignity will rise to instigate such aberrations, and morning, noon, and night there will be fear and trembling, no one occupying a peaceful situation. But perhaps they will regard with awe the Heavenly warning, and solemnly cultivate sagely virtue, to such an extent as the present case. And so we officials in charge have been commanded, within the houses of the deities of our local regions, all reverently to engage in this action and to send up reports in this manner. It is hoped that the diligent sincerity of our acts will within a reasonable time obliterate the catastrophe, so as to summon an auspicious response. The Primal Lord has in the past manifested his awesome divinity, bringing to an end the original evil, residing in the mysterious depths of his Truth, showing brilliant light as if actually present. I, in sincere accord with the purport of His Majesty's proclamation, have had the pure things offered, and humbly do I hope for the deity's acceptance of the pure aspiration of us, his subjects, so that he will extirpate the demonic force and accumulate for us blessings, protecting our Dynasty and all its dependencies. I, unworthy of my office, sincerely plead and promise to engage in this work urgently and to the utmost. Bowing my head, again bowing my head, respectfully this memorial is presented.   *DYJ* 21/9a–b

---

229 Judging by his name, the deity "Great Sage, the True Primal Lord of the Golden Tower" is from the Daoist pantheon. For the Daoist Jiao ritual, see Michael Saso, *Taoism and the Rite of Cosmic Renewal* (Pullman: Washington State University Press, 1972).

3   *An Account of the Cave of the Immortals*[230] *in Yangmo Valley in Miangu Subcounty, Lizhou County*

In the spring of the year *gengxu* [1070], I was returning to the court, and passed through Lizhou. Mr. Kou Yin, Gongfu, Circuit Judge, told me that recently, according to what was said by a native of Zhaotian Way-Station, at a distance of seven or eight *li*[231] from this place, among the cliffs and valleys there is a cave from which divine immortals have been seen to emerge. So he [probably Kou Yin] went to observe the site. From Dragon-Cave Tower he set out by boat and went down in a westerly direction, passing through a small gorge, and came upon a mountain powerfully jutting up as if ten thousand fathoms, blue-green cliffs looking as if they had been sliced, and in their midst yawned a great opening, perhaps fifty or sixty feet high.

At that moment, the sun was beaming down from a clear sky. Two young boys emerged from the cave, followed by a man in a white robe and black headcloth, dragging a stick behind, and with long beard hanging down, his lapels and sash flapping in the wind. He paced back and forth, gazing downward for a long while, accompanied now by several servants in blue robes. And there were creatures, something like chickens, or dogs, like tigers, or deer, gamboling before and after. In addition, there were attendants carrying fans and great parasols, the whole grandly solemn, just like a painting, and entirely enchanting. The tallest one among the group was over ten feet tall. Their deportment was slow and dignified, like that of ordinary gentlemen; they strolled about for a total distance of perhaps twenty or so *li*, and then disappeared.

When he [Kou] questioned the residents who lived below this mountain, they said that there was a tradition to the effect that during the Five Dynasties period [906–960], there was a local man of the surname Wang who planted crops beneath this mountain. His entire family was engaged in agriculture here. One day, he sent his wife out to get water; she drew the water, and on the way back home, encountered a sickly monk, whose body was covered with filthy sores, his flesh decomposed and stinking to such an extent that it was impossible to approach him. But he stepped forward and requested a drink. The wife was disgusted by

---

230 In China, especially in Daoism, caves are associated with Immortals. The idea that certain caves may be entrances to hidden magical realms is widespread.
231 A *li* is approximately a third of a mile, half a kilometer.

him, and terrified. In a flash, she dropped her carrying pole and ran away. The monk approached one of the vessels and drank, finishing nearly half, and then left. The wife, [returning,] had no way to change the water at this point, so she hid the truth of the affair and placed the water in the usual place in the fields. The family members, both young and old, came and drank, finishing the water. The wife, because of what had transpired, did not even wet her lips. That evening, when the wife brought the evening meal to the fields as usual, those who had drunk the water left over by the monk had all flown into this cave; the wife, not finding them, bawled and cried, ran about shouting and yelling, jumping wildly like a crazy person. Suddenly, she heard a voice from the cave, summoning her! The wife responded imploringly, but simply couldn't go there. She lived with anger and vexation until her death.

After this, firewood gathering boys and old men tending flocks became accustomed to seeing them [the Wang family, presumably transformed into Immortals], and did not even think it that strange. In recent years, whenever the sky would open and clear after a rainfall, they would emerge. And once emerged, they would inevitably spend the whole day in the central mountains. At times when flora and trees were blooming at their height, this was when they would come out most frequently.

Kou next took out a painting [of the Immortals] to show to me, and I said, "I have read the *Account of the Feng and Shan Sacrifices,* and I note that in the Xiangfu period [1008–1016], Inspector of Transportation for the Luzhou Circuit, Li Yunyuan submitted a memorial to the effect that in Yangmo Valley of Miangu Subcounty, divine Immortals appeared from a mountain cave. He said that he himself had traveled there and seen them, three times in all. Some of those who emerged just stood there, others walked about, their robes and garments all producing a wondrous glow. Only at sunset did they disappear." This, of course, refers to this very place.

I therefore asked for a second version of the painting that Kou had, and brought it back with me. In the autumn of the year *renzi* [1072], I was transferred to the position of Magistrate of Xingyuan, and there was a certain Jia Junxuan, an official in Xinfu, who came from Nanrong to visit me at Lingyang. When he saw the painting, displayed on a screen, he told me that when he had formerly held office at Yangzhou, he frequently collaborated with Lu Pi, the Doctor of Letters of the Supreme Norm Academy, in examining [potential] *jinshi* candidates at Ningwu, and there he too heard of this. Once, on the appointed day of return, he and Pi visited the very cave, and stood there together for a long time, and what they saw indeed in no way gave the lie to the account. They pointed to the streams and gullies, peaks, ridges, streams, valleys and stone pathways in the painting, twisting and turning, appearing and disappearing, and said that in every detail they corresponded to the actual place. At a gathering at the residence of Master Yu Zhiyan, I unrolled the painting and commissioned a craftsman to copy it, so that I would be able to record the whole matter, and inscribe it on the copy. Hence I have written this account, recorded on the twenty-third day of the ninth month.

DYJ 22/4a–5a

4   *How Mr. Hu of Pengzhou Thrice Encountered Uncanny Men*

In the spring of the sixth year of *xining* [1073], I was lodging at Tianpeng. The monk Minxing, Wuyan,[232] of the Chengtian district of Chengdu, was there as well. He related to me how in the northern area of the city, there was a certain Mr. Hu, personal name Chao, courtesy name Yitian, who was known at the beginning of our dynasty as a man of great wealth who cultivated the accumulation of good deeds. He donated to a temple where he resided for a while, images of foreign monks, the Four Deva Kings,[233] and Luohans. After this, a proclamation came down to the effect that Yitian should go to the capital, where he would be presented with an official position. But Yitian had no desire to be an official, and so declined. He did go to the capital, where he spent some time going out and visiting places. As for the date when his return home to the west [Chengdu] would be ordered, he daily predicted to his family that it would be on [one of the eight] Kingly Days,[234] and when the day was announced, sure enough it was, without the slightest discrepancy.

---

232 For Minxing, courtesy name Wuyan, see also prose nos. 5 and 8, and poem 131.
233 The Four Deva Kings are guardians of the four directions. Luohans, *arhats* in Sanskrit, are "worthy ones," well advanced on the path to Buddhist perfection.
234 The Eight Kingly Days are the start of spring 立春, the spring equinox 春分, the start of summer 立夏, the summer solstice 夏至, the start of autumn 立秋, the autumn equinox 秋分, the start of winter 立冬, and the winter solstice 冬至. Various *sutras* indicate that these are particularly auspicious days on which to practice austerities such as fasting, as all the protective deities, including the Four Deva Kings, come forth to guard the devout on these days.

At the beginning of this journey, when Yitian had departed from Peng, along the entire route until he reached the capital, people would frequently see a Man of the Way, wearing a tattered serge garment, but strangely magnificent in personal appearance, routinely at the side of Yitian. Suddenly, someone asked Yitian whether he was not able to see this man, but upon being spoken to, Yitian simply smiled and did not answer. This was indeed because he knew within himself that the Deva Kings were secretly guarding and supporting him.

A certain fortune-teller once told Yitian that he would never live beyond the age of forty, so Yitian went on an excursion to Mount Hua to visit Xiyi, Master Chen [Tuan].[235] The Master was absolutely delighted to meet him, and Hu remained with him for a long time. Chen concocted for him a cauldronful of special herbs, and told him to take it home with him, and to imbibe the contents. After this, he instructed him in techniques for extending one's years and transcending the world. Yitian, returning home, followed these teachings in full. After a lengthy period of this, his body became weightless, as if he were about to go flying off with the wind, and rising upwards. His fellow townsmen marveled at this.

One day, someone knocked at his gate. When Yitian sent someone to check, the man was unable to see anyone. All he could find was a set of seventeen staffs, leaning against the gateway, which the visitor had left there before disappearing. Yitian took them in, but couldn't figure out why they had been left for him. After this incident, Hu Yitian's household and family flourished to an even greater extent, passing on their good fortune to generations, continuing to the present day. Yitian finally died, having reached the age of seventy-eight.

Together with Minxing, I went to visit his home, and there we saw the staffs and some herbal medicine that also was mentioned. The staffs were made of a type of wood yet unknown in the world, of a purplish color, hard and smooth, and entirely attractive. The medicine consisted

---

235 Chen Tuan is generally revered as one of the greatest Daoist practitioners. It is interesting that a devout Buddhist such as Hu Chao would also consult with Daoist masters, but such is the eclecticism often characteristic of Chinese religion. Chen is said to have died in 989, so he would have been a contemporary of Hu. Livia Kohn calls attention to the assimilation of Chen's cult to Buddhism, especially in the Huangbo school founded in China but with a major development in Japan (called Ōbaku) after masters of the school moved there to evade the Manchu conquest in the later seventeenth century. See poem 148 and note, and 10 below.

of pills the size of crossbow pellets, reddish-yellow and giving off a glow, and hidden within were various gems, the heft of gold or jade.

I sighed, and said, "Yitian was a man we cannot fully understand; he engaged in secret practices hard to fathom. And that must be why three such uncanny men would make a regular practice of meeting with him. He must have impressed and inspired them to such an extent! Although Yitian has departed this world, he must certainly still be wandering with these men beyond the realm of dust! How could anyone take him for an ordinary, vulgar person?"

Yitian's grandson, Hu Jing, is himself a *jinshi* degree holder, upright, deep, and of profound elegance. He is praised throughout the town. I therefore spoke thus to Minxing: "Jing is an outstanding scholar. Thus we see how the children and grandchildren of the Hu lineage have continued the glorious numinousness of their grandsire, generations in an auspicious sequence, without any end in sight." To which Minxing replied, "That is so. This must be recorded!"

After I came to Xingyuan, Hu Jing sent a man one thousand *li* with a letter requesting an account to be written. I have recorded this one for him. *DYJ* 22/5b–6b

5   An Account of the Paintings of Master Zhang of Pengzhou

Sichuan has been a place of many outstanding craftsmen, ever since the two emperors of Tang took refuge there[236] and brought as part of their entourage Imperial Painting Intendants. Therefore, preserved in the temple precincts of all the various districts of Chengdu and environs are images of Buddhas, Bodhisattvas, Luohans, etc., of such a number that other places in the world, although they certainly can be said to possess many ancient remains, are not as rich in this type of art as is this region. After this, passing through the Two Usurpations[237] to the beginning of the present dynasty, the wellsprings of this art were not very deep, although works which can be called superb examples of [Buddhist?] painting do

---

236 Tang Xuanzong, or Minghuang, and his son, later to become Emperor Suzong, who fled to Sichuan after 755.

237 Probably a reference to the two brief dynasties, the Former Shu and Latter Shu, which ruled Sichuan during the Five Dynasties period (906–960), with the implication that they were illegitimate.

appear intermittently. But the practice in recent times has been shallow and vulgar, and there is a void in which we hear no names of great artists. This is for no other reason but this: that the artisans of the time have simply been for profit, and have not put the emphasis on the craft they are practicing.

It is Master Zhang of Tianpeng alone who has been able to continue the study of a true man of the Way, using his brush and applying colors with spirit-resonance and exemplary composition, never for a moment simply allowing himself to get sloppy. He was single-mindedly devoted to the finest techniques, never being seduced by the mindset of worldly vulgarity. Indeed, he is to be admired!

I lodged at Peng for several months, and had a good deal of leisure during this period, so every day, together with Minxing, the monk of Chengtian, I viewed and enjoyed nearly every work from the hand of Master Zhang. Truly, there is no other man capable of comparing with him in any way! As it happens, Minxing is his secular descendant [i.e., his secular surname, relinquished upon becoming a monk, was Zhang, and he is descended from him]. Minxing is outstandingly brilliant and comprehensively knowledgable, and is himself expert at this art! When he learned that I so appreciated the works of his ancestor, he rubbed off a rock surface [so it could be inscribed] and requested that I speak of how this came to be the case. Recorded on an autumn day, sixth year of *xining* [1073].   DYJ 22/6b–7a

6   *An Account of the Painting of the Sixth Patriarch in the*
     Śūraṅgama Cloister in Chengdu

The monk Weizhong, courtesy name Huiya [980–1045] was originally affiliated with the Kaiyuan Temple in Pengzhou. He later traveled to Chengdu, and did not return to his native land for a period of forty years. By nature, he was solitary and upright, and would not rashly associate with others. He was expert at Chan [meditation] and Vinaya [rules of monastic conduct] studies, and was expert at composing poetry in a style pure and wholesome. His fellow monks admired him. He did have an occasional friendship with Kepeng, often calling him his "Uncle in poetry." (Kepeng was a Sichuan monk who was good at poetry.) In addition, he was conversant with the books of our Scholars' Learning [i.e., Confucianism]. Should any student approach him with questions about the meaning of anything, they would find sunlight flooding the area beneath his seat, while he himself had an emaciated body, dirty face, tattered robe, and shoes split open, so that his visitors could not at first realize what great abilities he held within. In worldly years, he reached the age of sixty, and then expired at the Sweet Dew sacred locale. This took place on the ninth day of the fifth month, fifth year of the Qingli period—an *yiyou* year [June 26, 1045].

Prior to his death, Weizhong completely "emptied his sack," [donated all his possessions] obtaining eighty thousand cash, entrusting it to his frequent companion, the Śūraṅgama Man of the Way, Master Jishu, saying, "I am about to depart. Whatever remains from my life, is merely this. Would you please commission on my behalf a craftsman of remarkable skill to paint the icon of the Sixth Patriarch [Huineng, 638–713] in the Śākyamuni Hall of your temple [the Śūraṅgama Cloister]? I would not presume to decline this project, even if it led to my being spat upon and cursed! What is more, I wish for pilgrims to view this icon, to realize the truth of this mind-heart, thus obtaining *darśana* [viewing of a sacred icon or person] and knowledge, and becoming capable of extirpating all fallacies, exterminating worldly signs, and forgetting the worldly mind-heart. Such is the meaning of the meritorious deed I wish to perform."

The Man of the Way agreed to this. At the time, a certain Liu Yunwen[238] of Guanghan was famed in his day [for painting Buddhist subjects], with extraordinary brilliance in the color and ornamentation, as well as perfect compositional structure. Master Jishu called upon him, and entrusted him with the task, emphasizing the deep, secret significance of the subject. And thus, "One flower produced five leaves,"[239] all mutually illuminating each other, indeed, a great karmic event in the Garden of the Dharma, as well as a contribution worthy of the rating Excellent Class from painting critics.

---

238 Liu Yunwen is recorded in *Tuhui baojian* (edition of the *Meishu congkan*, Vol. 2 [Taipei, 1964]), p. 179 close to the entry for Minxing.

239 "One flower with five leaves" is a frequently cited Chan (Zen) phrase, variously interpreted, but referring to the emergence of five schools or sects of Chan from the origin with Buddha himself, through Bodhidharma, the First Patriarch. It was Bodhidharma who brought the Chan school to China from India, leading to the development of the five schools and a succession of patriarchs, of whom Huineng was the sixth. The phrase was first used, apparently, in the *Jingde Chuandeng lu* (*Jingde Era* [1004–1007] *Record of the Transmission of the Lamp*), compiled by the monk Daoyuan in 1004. This phrase is often the subject of calligraphic works by Chan monks both in China and Japan.

I once had the opportunity to discuss with Weizhong the overarching meaning of the Five Classics; I held him in great esteem. At the time that the painting was being executed, I also had the opportunity to observe Yunwen apply his brush. It is now seventeen years later—I have successfully petitioned to leave the position of Editor of the Imperial Library, and to return home to serve my parents. I have been able to meet with [The Man of the Way] in Linqiong Commandery, and he asked me to record this, engraved in stone. Written on the fifteenth day of the fifth month of the sixth year of the Jiayou period—a *xinchou* year [June 5, 1061] in the Fangzhou Pavilion of the Eastern Garden.   *DYJ*, 22/7b–8a

7   *An Account of a Divine Dream*

In Xingyuan there is a Tang'an Temple, and in the temple a Hall of the Dais for Conferring Ordinations, in which is a Six-Armed Guanshiyin,[240] the Boddhisattva of Great Compassion, and this image was restored by the Lady Zhu of Ch'ang'an County, wife of Lu Hong, Huizhi, Adjudicator of Military Affairs and Secretary to the Household of the Crown Prince.

Prior to this, the Lady, for a period of five years starting in the *gengxu* year of the Xining period [1070], was to all intents and purposes pregnant, but unable to deliver! The Lady day and night lived in fear of what is known in the world as praying and petitioning the gods, and she and her husband would only use medical methods of treatment leading to a cure. There was not an instant that they did not fully engage in this. When it came to the *guichou* year [1073], in winter, Huizhi was transferred to Langzhong. One evening, the Lady unexpectedly dreamed that she journeyed to a great temple, and was walking through the corridors of the main hall. There she saw a deteriorated image, lying near the wall. The gilt and colors were dark and chipped, the hands and feet were all damaged. The Lady stood there, lamenting, for a long time. There appeared an old man, hair all white, who came to her and commented, "This potential meritorious deed has been witnessed by untold thousands of persons, and yet so far not one of them has been willing to undertake the restoration!" The Lady responded, "I, your child, unfortunately for

---

240 See also Chün-fang Yü, *Kuan-yin . . .* (op. cit.). I am further indebted to Prof. Robert Gimello for his help in interpreting some of the technical Buddhist terms in this piece.

Six-Armed, Eleven-Headed Guanyin. Cloth banner, ink and color on silk, painting proper 39 3/16 x 24 3/4 in (99.6 x W. 62.8 cm) dated 985. Harvard Art Museums/Arthur M. Sackler Museum.

years have had an unborn embryo in my womb; I am ignorant of the distinction between good and evil, and yet I would undertake the restored ornamentation of this image, so as to lean upon its great power to make possible my giving birth as soon as I can. Would this be possible?" The old man responded, "If your fruits are such [i.e., if you do this], you will obtain divine recompense." With this she awoke. Upon her telling the dream to her husband Huizhi, they realized that there was no way of knowing *where* the image was, nor how they could get to see it.

In the twelfth month [of the next year], I and Huizhi visited a temple whose name violates the tabooed name of Empress Yide [941–975; the temple may well have been named Yide Temple 懿德寺]. We happened to visit one of the buildings of this temple in which there was an old sculpture, lying there decaying in a side-chamber. I then summoned the Abbot and queried him, whereupon Huizhi suddenly exclaimed, "This is just like the one my wife dreamed about, every detail precisely as she described them to me!" He then returned home and told his wife about this, and she said, "It certainly seems like it!" So they went together to view the image, and she said, "Yes, that's it!"

With this, they selected an auspicious day, and moved the image to the front verandah. They commissioned a craftsman, following their instructions, to clean it of the slightest iota of dirt and dust, and to repair each and every bit of damage. After not many days, everything was precisely correct, with superb detailing throughout, one hundred blessings-worth of sheer beauty!

The local people came in droves to circumambulate the image, sighing in admiration.

The night after restoration of the image, the Lady dreamed once again of the old man, who approached her holding a spoonful of herbal medicine. This he gave her, saying "You may boil this, and then drink it." She did precisely that. For a long time she felt a constriction in her lower throat, and then she vomited out innumerable large and small objects black and white in color, and spit blood that was the color of coal. After several such episodes, she suddenly awoke, with sweat pouring in rivulets over her whole body; and her body seemed to relax, as if it had been relieved of a great burden. The next day, Huizhi came quickly to visit me with the happy news, "Yes, at last it has happened!"[241]

---

241 A similar account is given by Hong Mai (1123–1202) in his famous book of stories about strange and supernatural events, the *Yi Jian zhi* (*Matters Recorded by Master Yi*

I have heard that this Great One [Guanyin], formerly as many aeons ago as there are sands in the Ganges River, was engaged in observing the voices of the world [crying out in suffering]. With the "Proof of the Marvelous Dharma," heard from the Such-Come One [Buddha], he obtained the Two Supreme Wonders: above, together with all the Buddhas of the Ten Directions to share the power of compassion, and below, together with all the sentient beings to share compassion for them; above, to apply this wondrous power effortlessly in all forms of fearlessness, and in the observation of voices [crying out in suffering], and below to apply it to the salvation of all who suffer. And truly, if he did not sincerely supplicate in firm faith, deep and incisive, how could he in this way be so moved by people's yearnings, and with such wondrous wisdom achieve the supreme joy?

Because the Lady was herself so utterly sincere in her wish, and diligently engaged in the affairs of Buddha, not only have her demons and evil influences, wishing to cause her harm, today been completely obliterated and dispersed, but from this time forward, she will certainly obtain great blessings, and the auspiciousness of wisdom, beyond the shadow of a doubt.

Ah! If only those in the world lost in delusion, perverted in heart, slovenly and slothful in their lives, could come and view this sacred icon, how could there not be born in them the mind-heart of faith, how could they not return to the Good Way? They would benefit themselves, and benefit others, and such is the good *karma* than which nothing is greater.

Huizhi asked me to record this matter, and have it carved in stone, so that it might be placed beside the icon itself. Recorded on the fifteenth day of the fifth month of the eighth year of the Xining period—an *yimao* year [June 30, 1075].   *DYJ*, 22/8a–10a

---

Jian). He tells of an "old village woman" whose injured arm is miraculously healed when she arranges for the repair of a Guanshiyin image with a damaged arm. See Alister D. Inglis, *Hong Mai's Record of the Listener and Its Song Dynasty Context* (Albany: State University of New York Press, 2006), p. 151.

8   *Preface on Seeing Off Minxing, Wuyan*[242]

My relationship with the book *Zhuangzi* is that I read it for years. I loved how he [Master Zhuang] was so excellent at dynamically conveying his high-toned discourse, completely encompassing all the things and affairs of the world, with the inner principle of an expert prognosticator capturing the individual nature of all things. I once said of him, "Although indeed we have here a scholar of free-wheeling discourse, there is certainly not the slightest ground for actually accepting the truth of what he says."

It was afterward that I encountered the monk Master Sengzhao's[243] four great *Discussions*, and from them was enlightened to the concept of "[things] not really changing," and "[things] not truly existing," as well as to the meaning of "nonexistent knowledge," and "nonexistent names." Thus I became able gradually to reduce evil emotions, and directly to grasp the wondrous wisdom. When I now looked back at the doctrines of "free-and-easy wandering," and "the relativity of all things," which previously I had admired, oh, how petty and contentious they now seemed! And as for their having heights that could never be trod, and depths that could never be plummeted [i.e., Zhuangzi's ideas seemed merely fantastical], I now took the liberty of considering these to be disastrous flaws.

Then the Monk-Lecturer Wuyan came from Chengdu. And for me he established the Ladder to the Extinction of Karma, and extended the Rope that Extirpates Fallacies, enabling me to relax and free myself, to call upon the Non-Ultimate, and to reach the point where within the time of a single breath, Void and Form would all disappear. So great has been the power of Wuyan's influence upon me! And what level of gift can one say this is that I have thus received from him?

---

242 Wen Tong presents here what amounts to an account of a conversion experience, from Daoism to Buddhism. It is often said that in China, everyone followed each of the Three Teachings (Confucianism, Daoism, Buddhism), without conflict. But on the deepest level, one indeed finds cases of conflict in the minds of individual persons, leading to conversions amongst the three. See also poem131.

243 One of the foundational figures in the history of Chinese Buddhism, Sengzhao (384–414) is described by Arthur F. Wright in his *Buddhism in Chinese History* (Stanford University Press, 1959, p. 135) as the author of "one of the most important Chinese Buddhist texts," which includes his "discussions," referred to by Wen Tong, on such matters as "things not changing" (because their being is so tenuous that there really is nothing there to change), and "things not truly existing." Sengzhao's master was the greatest of translators of Buddhist texts from Sanskrit into Chinese, Kumārajīva (343/344–413).

One day, Wuyan suddenly spoke to me of his plan to return to the West; repeatedly did I grab hold of his robe and urge him to stay, but to no avail. And so I wrote this to send him in parting, and to show something of my thoughts. Written on a *jiashen* day in the last month of winter of the sixth year of Xining—a *guichou* year [1073–early 1074].

DYJ, 26/5a–b

9 *Preface on the Daoist, Yuan Weizheng, Courtesy Name, Xingzhi*

The Daoist Master Yuan is a man of Langzhong. The shrine where he resides is only a hundred *li* from my Mount Tai mountain residence. Formerly, when I was in my hometown, I had already heard of Master Yuan, and how he was able to employ the Sixty-four Hexagrams to penetrate the Five Elements, accompany the Six Deities, and manipulate the Seventy-two Malignancies, to predict people's good or ill fortune, obtaining a response even before any omens had been manifested. And in each and every detail, it was as if he had seen the outcome with his own eyes. But I had not yet had the opportunity of meeting Master Yuan.

After this, when I held the office of Secretary in the Imperial Library, I had the good fortune to associate with high-level scholar-officials. And daily there were frequently those who would tell me that the Daoist Master came from Sichuan, and was expert at using the hexagram lines and images to obtain knowledge of good and evil outcomes, a man of the same ilk as Guo Jingchun or Guan Gongming [famed prognosticators of the past].

But although I had thus heard for a long time about how superb were the arts of Master Yuan, I still would not have presumed therefore to seek out Master Yuan for a dialogue with him.

One day of leisure, I was enjoying the coolness at a Daoist shrine south of the capital, when a Daoist emerged from the western verandah, with high cheekbones and a broad forehead, extremely striking and dignified in appearance. I therefore took the liberty of entering and sitting in the hall beside him and I asked him where he came from. To which he replied, "I am from Sichuan." Then I asked him how he came to be residing in this place, and he answered, "Some years ago, in my prognostications I happened to obtain an outcome involving men of power and high station. And sure enough, happily, [well-wishers] memorialized on my behalf so that [the court] conferred upon me a purple robe [a great honor for religious figures], and housed me here." With this, I asked him who had been his master, such that his arts were of this caliber, and he said, "At the time I resided in Sichuan, I already received from an uncanny man a secret text. Then I traveled around throughout the world, east, west, south and north, virtually everywhere, and if I heard that at such-and-such a place there was such-and-such a man expert at these arts, even if that place were several thousands of *li* away, I would inevitably go there to inquire from him. Thus I firmed up my studies, and subsequently was without any doubts whatsoever. Today, no matter what is asked of me, it is as easy for me as [in Zhuangzi's accounts of] a master butcher's knife slicing effortlessly through a whole ox, or a master archer's arrowhead piercing a flea from far off: I see it all with sudden, complete clarity." And so I realized, this was none other than the Master Yuan of whom I had heard when in my hometown, and of whom more recently the scholar-officials at court had been telling me.

I therefore began to associate with him, visiting back and forth. One day he called upon me, and he said that friends all call each other by their courtesy names, but "I alone have not presumed to do so." He asked me to give him a courtesy name, and I said, "I take it that Weizheng [惟正, literally, 'to be orthodox'] is your personal name? Now, adhering to the 'orthodox' is the proper path to the establishment of the Way. Between Heaven and Earth, all those who involve themselves in the actual practice of such arts [as yours] must in every case protect their inner purity in order to perfect the application [of these arts]. If not, and they lose control, they will fall into perverse and wrongful ways [black magic], chaotic confusion and aberrational inclination towards evil, without any exception. Now you, sir, are now famous in your day for these arts, and you have the trust of people. If you can continue to *carry them out* [xingzhi, 行之] in accordance with the orthodox, and to protect your purity, so as absolutely never to allow a desire for mere profit to disturb your mind, to be just like Yan Ziping and Sima Jizhu [two admired prognosticators of old] in your actions, then your Way will indeed be noble. You must take Xingzhi as your courtesy name [so that personal name and courtesy name together will mean, "To carry out based on the orthodox way"]. Master Yuan went down on his knees, and said, "I, a man who has lived outside the normal realm of affairs, have never heard such words as these! How fortunate that you, sir, have now given me a courtesy name, how could I presume not to admire you until the end of my days?"

I have written this down to present to him. Respectfully written as a preface, on the first day of the fifth year of the Jiayou period—a *gengzi* year [February 5, 1060].   *DYJ*, 26/6b–7b

10   *Written After a Poem by Master Xiyi Shrine of Heavenly Blessings in Qiongzhou*

Master Xiyi, Chen Tuan,[244] courtesy name Tunan, in the Tianfu period of the Latter Jin Dynasty [936–43], traveled here to Sichuan. He had heard that in this county [Qiongzhou], at the Shrine of the Heavenly Master, a certain He Chang'yi, Abbot of Majesty, possessed a Daoist technique, such that he was expert at suspending his breath, while his inner essence would go flying abroad into the vastness. Once he put his head down on the pillow, it might be over a month before he would awaken. And so Chen Tuan stayed at this shrine to study with him, and finally mastered the technique. He then returned to the region Within-the-Pass, where his cultivation of the technique became even more advanced. He was able to slough off the aging body and take on the movements of a child as if he were a divinity. Emperor Taizong [of the Song dynasty, r. 976–997] often summoned him to court to ask questions of him, and expressed his will that Chen be presented with a poem [by the Emperor] as well as an honorific cognomen [Master Xiyi, or Master of What is Inaudible and Invisible], and finally released him to reside at Mount Hua [the Western Sacred Mountain]. Here, in his manifestation of spiritual powers he displayed wonders. After a long while, he was liberated from this earthly realm. Right up to the present day, all people within the four seas who possess teeth and tongues, including illiterate old geezers and boorish youths, are able to recount the doings of the Master in their full brilliance.

The Master was in fact originally a scholar [i.e., of the Confucian classics], but once he became a follower of the Void and Empty, all of the poems he wrote made their way into the worldly realm, where they were able to open the ears of the deaf, and scrape motes, opening the eyes of the blind, the pathways through their deeper passages being easy to negotiate. As soon as one of his poems fell into the dusty world, even

---

244 It should be noted that although the dates of Chen Tuan are now regarded as being ca. 920–989, as given by Livia Kohn (see note to poem 148), in popular legend he was already regarded in Wen Tong's day as having lived over one hundred years.

ordinary folks in the marketplace would chant them out loud, ceaselessly, feeling as if they too could personally travel to the secret regions of the True Gateway.

At that time, there was one poem[245] which he presented to Chang'yi [his teacher], and he inscribed it in his own calligraphy upon one of the pillars of the main hall of the shrine. Later men, however, were already worrying that the ink might be effaced, so they engraved it. But even so, in the course of the years, many holes formed. (From the year *dingyou* [937] to the present time, indeed 114 years have passed.) Moss overgrew it, dust darkened it, and it became obscured and blackened. This continued through several regimes, none of which paid any attention. Then, in the year *gengyin* of the Huangyou period [1050], Master Cui[246] of Boling took office as Commander of the local commandery. The year after that, his official duties slackening off, he had leisure time to indulge himself in the pleasure of pursuing wondrous matters, and upon studying a gazetteer, he came upon a reference to this [calligraphy by Chen Tuan of his own poem]. And so he immediately went there, to examine it for himself. Upon reading it, he sighed, saying, "Are these not the words of one who has distanced himself from physical form, and put away all servile, tool-like service? Put aside fame and official hat-strings, escaped from bowing down for benefit to himself? Is this not one capable of helping a man to achieve the Great Crossroad? Would not that which an Achieved

---

245 The text of the poem by Chen Tuan is recorded in the influential anthology *Songshi jishi* (*Recording Matters Pertaining to Song Poetry*), Shanghai guji chubanshe, 1983, Vol. 1, p. 132, edited by Li E (1692–1752). The poem is a seven-character per line quatrain introduced by the poet's prose preface, and may be translated as follows:

As I was returning from having enjoyed myself at a little wine-gathering held by Secretary Yin Shuinan, the Magistrate, I relaxed my reins and knocked at a pine-gate, there to visit His Noble Excellency [He Chang'yi, his teacher]. *We passed the time with tea and talk, and I wrote, impromptu, twenty-eight words* [i.e., a seven-character per line quatrain]. *His disciple in the Gate of the Way, Tunan* [Chen Tuan] *presents this to him.*

I say floating glory is truly a delusion:
Drunk, I relax my reins to call on His Noble Excellency!
Since I've heard the principles of his Mysterious Discourse,
       so dark and deep,
I've come to feel the whole dusty world
       is nothing but a dream.

246 Master Cui is possibly Cui Kuang (1015–1099), a Boling man. His epitaph was composed by Su Shi's disciple and friend, the important poet Zhang Lei (1052–1112).

Man holds within be profoundly like this? But alas, the pillar may rot away, and thus one will not be able to preserve it for future generations! Perhaps if it were cut in stone, that might serve the case." And so he sought to have the calligraphy copied [in stone]. And then he addressed Wen Tong [myself] who was on his staff at the time: "Could you, sir, write a systematic account of the history of this, so that visitors may know what is involved? Then we would be able to bequeath it to future generations in perpetuity. Such is the plan of my office." I, Tong, said, "Yes sir!" and respectfully took hold of my writing brush, willing to lay out the rough details, while holding in reverence that which has inspired His Excellency. This is surely superior to blocking the good so that it can never be communicated for thousands of years. Written on the day of the *zhongyuan* festival [February 28, 1051].   *DYJ* add/*xia*, 1b–2b.

Documents on Praying for Rain (or the End of Excessive Rainfall) and Related Matters

11   *Receiving an Imperial Command to Pray for Rain while Sacrificing to Mount Zhongliang*[247]

On such-and-such a day of such-and-such a year, because of a prolonged absence of rainfall and subsequent drought, the court commanded that the local magistrates each within his region *personally* offer sincere prayers. I respectfully undertook an excursion to Mount Zhongliang, where I offered sacrifice to such-and-such a deity [the deity of the mountain], stating the following:

> "From the imperial domains unto all the provinces of the dynasty, and from last winter unto the present autumn, the evil Drought Demon has freely unleashed his destructive harm. For the common folk, this has meant a lack of timely rainfall, leading to the destruction of all crops, and the failure of the great fields, and to extreme difficulty for the people in finding food, and massive numbers of them taking to the roads, without any other recourse. The Son of Heaven, deeply feeling their suffering, was moved

---

247 Mount Zhongliang is in the Chongqing region, then included in Sichuan.

to trembling solicitude, day and night earnestly commiserating. He was harsh with his honorable self, submitting himself to self-denial, and profoundly berating himself in the hope of calling upon [the deities] high and low. And yet for a long time there was no response. And so he examined himself to discover what fault of heart there might be in him, as earnestly as if he were burning within. He sent messengers throughout the realm with instructions that they 'should not sacrifice to any but real gods.' Such was his sincerity! And yet, in the end, there was no recompense. Still, he considered that perhaps there were some shrines to mountain spirits that might have been overlooked, and so he condescended to extend his actions to the common folk so that they too could participate. He therefore issued a special proclamation, commanding local officials to visit those places within their jurisdictions that had deities listed in the official records, and there *personally* to offer the good things to eat in sacrifice to gods starting with those of the 'melted' and 'congealed' [bodies of water and mountains], and extending to those in charge of [weather in the] Liang and Han regions—all the magnificent, great townships near and far—his honored gaze falling upon streams and valleys opening on all sides, and embracing at great distance woods and copses, where wind and thunder lie hidden and in storage, and clouds and fog come spitting forth, so that, although the harvest may have been delayed because of drought, there would certainly be something, at least, to be harvested.

"Now the Son of Heaven takes control of the counties with bodies of water, none of them evading his comprehensive rulership, these being the homes of deities. And this means that gods who lord it over localities must exhaust themselves as well in attending to this matter, so as to dispel the sadness of the Son of Heaven above, and to beseech the Lord on High that we may all perform our duties, and universally bring fructifying moisture, thus saving all from this catastrophe through His great commands. This is the excellent meritorious work and flourishing virtue through which the gods may serve the Lord on High and support the Son of Heaven, as well as show their love for the common folk on a grand scale and over vast distances, not only limited to one petty little locality. Such is the brilliant intelligence of the deities, that they must certainly embody the will of the Son of Heaven to this effect [saving the land from drought]. What need is there for local officials to presume further to annoy their staffs with irksome words of exhortation?"   *DYJ* 35/1a–2a

12   *Text on Sacrificing at the Shrines of all the Various Spirits*

For several years now, Heaven and Earth have undergone great aberrational transformations, heard of in the various provinces, and quite frequently. His Majesty, therefore, in awed solicitude has cultivated self-examination, exhorting himself to virtue and diligently engaging himself in governance, so as to discover a way that he might touch the hearts of deities and spirits, leading to auspicious response on behalf of the ordinary people, thus assuaging the suffering of the common folk, and yet these perversions and evil aberrations could not be repressed.

Thus now, the Star Patterns are manifesting warning signs, some of which have terrified people through sights and sounds. In this current measure [probably the Emperor's pardoning of all criminals, followed by the Imperial Command discussed in the previous document], reaching extensively to all who are hidden away, no matter how far they may be, His Majesty pardons all hidden wrongs, allays all grievances, so that each and every one will be cleansed and alleviated, with an end to receive auspicious blessings, and, above, to answer the manifest reprimands [of Heaven]. All of this then led to his commanding the local officials of the world, guided by the focused purity of His Majesty's will, to offer brilliant sacrifices in the spirit-shrines within their territories, and all of us together obliterate the evil and recover the good.

My own goal is respectfully to serve and cultivate my official duties, as close as possible to the deities. May they hear this.   *DYJ* 35/2a

13   *Text on Sacrificing to the Gods of Zitong County*[248]

The gods being intelligent and correctly straightforward, they receive offerings from this land, through their spiritual powers displaying wonders such that the people of Sichuan are awed by them and hold them in reverence.

I herewith am in receipt of a brilliant proclamation commanding that I take over the governance of Renshou, a realm of one thousand *li* square. I indeed have taken office there. Nevertheless, consoling the weak and the good, suppressing the powerful and cruel, and promulgating educational transformation, regulating all vulgar practices—within two years of such governance, the well-being of this district has been achieved, and this is entirely the accomplishment of the responsible Inspector. How could a man not possessed of great talent and ability ever have achieved such things? As for myself, by nature and in my thinking I am lowly and abased, ignorant of the principles of even low-level governance. Thus in my temporary occupation of this office, attempting to carry out such projects, I fear that I am not up to the task, and that I therefore have betrayed the virtue of His Majesty, bringing in recompense calamity to those below. This is something over which I have trembled in fear day and night, devoutly wishing that the gods would secretly end their silence, leading to their timely conferral of salutary warnings, and correct thoughts in my mind, and correct words spoken by my lips, so I may never fall again into such fallacious errors as before.

But, given the court's reason for sending me here to Lingzhou, and the reason of the residents of Lingzhou for placing their hopes in my tenure here, and at the same time, given my drinking and eating, acting and resting, one actually cannot hope I deserve a response from such as the deities.   *DYJ*, 35/6a

---

248 Zitong County is Wen Tong's hometown, northeast of Chengdu, Sichuan Province.

14-18 *Five Texts on Praying for Rain*

i [祭] 玉女 [文]²³

惟神稟大霄清眞之靈而天下所謂溪谷淵泉
者神寔主之惟是玉井之勝蹟殊利郡志所載
皆神之化力使然旣已是惠養於一方其爲福
於斯民也厚矣乃今其地苦此旱熯神顧忍視
之哉叢陰漬潤頃刻萬里在神之翩然飛空勅
諸群龍也監此丹素願神行之

i *Text on Sacrificing to the Jade Lady*²⁵⁰

Now you, the Deity, have been endowed by the Spirit of the Purified Truth of the Great Empyrean, and yet what are known as the rivers, valleys, abysses, and waterfalls of this world below are in fact ruled by you, and especially advantageous has been the wondrous site of the Jade Well.²⁵¹ Recorded in the provincial gazetteer [of Sichuan] are all manner of wonders, caused by your divine, transformational power. And it is because of this that you have enjoyed nurturement by means of offerings from this region. The blessings you have conferred upon this our people have been manifold.

But now, the soil here is thus parched and dried up. Can you, oh Goddess! bear to witness this? For fructifying moisture from all the clustered, shady places to expand over ten thousand *li* in just one instant, lies in your power: should you just fly off through the void, and issue a command to all the tribe of dragon deities!

Having examined this cinnabar writing on silk, may the Deity implement it!   *DYJ*, 35/6b

---

249 The first and last characters appear in the *Siku quanshu* edition but not in the Wanli edition of *DYJ*.

250 See also poem 49.

251 There is an Yujing xiang, or Jade Well Subcounty, in Sichuan, far to the northeast of Chengdu.

ii *Text on Sacrificing to the Lady of Sagacious Wisdom*[252]

It is the case that you, our Lady, once promised the Master of Methods that you would seek to protect this our region. Today, the *yang*-sun force is raging with drought, and the Many Crops are about to fail. Your Ladyship and your household are expert at sending thunder and rain: if you have not renounced your vow, and are prepared to save this, your people, may you command that this be done, and you will enjoy sacrifices by the people of this land. May you endure as long as Heaven and Earth! We will also present this matter to the Master of Methods, so that he need not feel ashamed.   *DYJ* 35/6b–7a

iii *Text on Sacrificing to the Heavenly King*[253]

Now the North is the land where the ten thousand things all originate, and all end. Of the noble deities of Heaven, many take their abode there, and your Majesty rules serenely over that land. You are the most highly praised for your sovereign might, and in all the cities and military posts, there are shrines wherein can be found your icon. The people too gaze up at you with reverence, seeking blessings from you. But now, this fierce, fiery heat is damaging the Many Crops. Your Majesty has power over clouds and rain, and it should be easy for you to command them, thus assuaging the wishes of the people. With this we take the liberty of bothering you for your attention to this matter.   *DYJ* 35/7a

iv *Text on Sacrificing to the Master of Methods*

Given that you, Master, have received the Primal Unitary Orthodox Energy, and have personally earned the Secret Certificate, in all cases [of evil spirits] presuming to send calamitous harm to the people below, should you, Master of Methods, impose your authority upon the deities, there will inevitably result a pacification and extirpation of the evil.

---

252 A temple to this goddess, Ruiwang Furen, in Chengdu was associated with successful prayers for rain. The goddess was originally known as the Dragon Lady, but was officially granted the title Lady of Sagacious Wisdom in gratitude for her responsiveness.
253 In his master's thesis Xiao Yuxia classifies the addressee of this text and the previous as "nature gods" (*ziran shen* 自然神), as opposed to "anthropomorphic gods" (*renge shen* 人格神), with no further explanation. Both, however, do seem vaguely personal, while the latter in particular may well be a local deity based upon an actual person. Xiao seems in any case to mean by the term "anthropomorphic," historical persons who were apotheosized upon death. See his *Songdai qiyuwen yanjiu* ("A Study of Song Dynasty Texts on Praying for Rain," Northwest Normal University, China, 2013), p. 46.

The people of this province have received your divine gifts, oh Master, for over one thousand years. At present, the drought has reached the point where the Demon is about to destroy utterly this year's harvest. Ah, Master of Methods! Please blow your spiritual breath upon our knives, spit forth rain from the waters: How could you possibly begrudge us one instant of your power? We yearn only to see you, just once, confer watery spray upon that which is all withered.   *DYJ* 35/7a–b

v A Text on Sacrificing to All the Deities

Long has been the time over which you have received sacrifices from the people of Lingzhou. And the people of Lingzhou, in looking reverently upwards toward the sovereign kindnesses of you deities have never dared to forget them for even a single day. And you deities, in taking note of this degree of loyalty on the part of the people of Lingzhou, ought to cogitate on how to recompense the sincerity of their offerings in sacrifice. Today, the people's fields are right in the middle of yearning for fructifying rainfall, and yet the winds are dry, the sun is searing, and this region is in a state of calamity. The people of Lingzhou are day and night looking for some sign of the heart of compassionate salvation on the part of you deities. One cannot even compare their yearning [for rainwater] to that of a miserable, landed fish lying in a dried-out wheel rut, or a thirsty beast running across a parched plain. Please send a deluge! Indeed it must be easy for you deities to employ your power.   *DYJ* 35/7b–8a

19   A Text on Thanking for Rainfall[254]

Formerly, as seasonal rains missed their time and the autumnal plantings were unable to be harvested, the local magistrates, feeling great solicitude for our people, and fearing they might encounter the disaster of great difficulty in finding food, rushed about to all the various spirit-shrines in the hope that you gods might spare the gift of a single downpour, thus showing compassion upon the people and saving them. And indeed you deities aided Heaven in nurturing and compassionately commiserating with them, pouring down the sweet moisture, so that plots of land were sufficiently watered, and the grains, hemp, rice, and other crops

---

254 The five texts indicated in the title preceding them have been presented; this seems to be an additional text thanking the gods for their responses to those.

flourished and grew healthily. Having received the help of you, the deities, we consider that there is no adequate way we can repay you. But at least we can compose this announcement, which is after all only the normal ceremonial procedure, and hope that you, the deities, may kindly take note of it, and bless us just this once with your presence as recipients of the sacrifice.

DYJ 35/8a

Paying respects at the partially renovated grave mound of Wen Tong, Yongtai-xiang in Yanting County, Sichuan, China.

Bibliography

This bibliography is limited to publications of significant relevance to this book. Other works are cited in the text or notes. For collections of Wen Tong's writings, see the Bibliographical Note, p 33.

Bush, Susan and Hsio-yen Shih. *Early Chinese Texts on Painting*. Cambridge, MA: Harvard University Press,1985.

Chang Bide 昌彼得 *et al. Songren zhuanji ziliao suoyin* 宋人傳記資料索引 *(An Index to Biographical Materials on People of the Song Dynasty)*, in six volumes. Taipei: Dingwen shuju, 1974–1976.

Chaves, Jonathan. *The Chinese Painter as Poet*. New York: China Institute in America, 2000.

_____. *Mei Yao-ch'en and the Development of Early Sung Poetry.* New York: Columbia University Press, 1976.

_____. *Singing of the Source: Nature and God in the Poetry of the Chinese Painter, Wu Li (1638–1712)*. Honolulu: University of Hawaii Press, 1993.

_____. "The Panoply of Images: A Reconsideration of the Literary Theory of the Kung-an School," in Christian Murck and Susan Bush, eds., *Chinese Theories of the Arts*. Princeton University Press, 1982.

_____. "'Traces Buried among the Market Towns': Literary Expressions of Reclusion," in Peter C. Sturman and Susan S. Tai, eds., *The Artful Recluse: Painting, Poetry, and Politics in Seventeenth-Century China*. Santa Barbara Museum of Art and DelMonico Books-Prestel, 2012.

Creel, Herlee. *What is Taoism? and Other Studies in Chinese Cultural History.* University of Chicago Press, 1970.

Frodsham, J. D. *The Poems of Li Ho.* Oxford: Clarendon Press, 1970; with multiple later reprints by various presses as *The Collected Poems of Li He.*

Gimello, Robert M. "Mārga and Culture: Learning, Letters, and liberation in Northern Sung Ch'an," in Robert E. Buswell, Jr. and Robert M. Gimello, eds., *Paths to Liberation: the Mārga and its Transformations in Buddhist Thought.* Honolulu: University of Hawaii Press, 1992.

Kohn, Livia. Entry on Chen Tuan in Fabrizio Pregadio, ed., *The Encyclopedia of Taoism.* in two volumes. Routledge, 2008.

Liu, James T. C. *Reform in Sung China: Wang An-shih (1021–1086) and His New Policies.* Cambridge, MA: Harvard University Press, 1959.

Pearson, Margaret J. *Wang Fu and the Comments of a Recluse,* a translation and study of the *Qianfu lun* 潛夫論 (*A Discourse on the Man Who's Hidden Away*), by Wang Fu 王符 (ca. 82–167). Tempe, AZ: Center for Asian Studies, Arizona State University, 1989.

Rudolph, Richard. "Preliminary Notes on Sung Archaeology," *Journal of Asian Studies*, Vol. 22 (1963).

Saso, Michael. *Taoism and the Rite of Cosmic Renewal.* Washington State University Press, 1972.

Song shi jishi 宋詩紀事 ("Recording Matters Pertaining to Song *Shi* Poetry") compiled by Li E 厲鶚 (1692–1752). Shanghai guji chubanshe, in two volumes, 1983.

Su Shi 蘇軾. *Dongpo qi ji* 東坡七集 (*Seven Collections of Dongpo's Writings*) edition of the *Sibu beiyao*, Vol. 2 40/6b.

Van Gulik, Robert. *The Gibbon in China: An Essay in Chinese Animal Lore.* Leiden: E.J. Brill, 1967.

Wang Fu, see Pearson, Margaret.

Watson, Burton, trans., Yoshikawa Kōjirō, *An Introduction to Sung Poetry.* Cambridge, MA: Harvard University Press, 1967.

_____. *Su Tung-p'o: Selections from a Sung Dynasty Poet.* New York: Columbia University Press, 1965; reprinted Copper Canyon Press, 1993.

Wright, Arthur F. *Buddhism in Chinese History.* Stanford University Press, 1959.

Wu Zhizhen 吳之振, et al., eds. *Song Shi chao* 宋詩鈔 *(Volumes of Song Shi Poetry),* in four volumes. Beijing: Zhonghua shuju, 1986.

Xiao Yuxia 肖[=蕭]玉霞, MA thesis. *Songdai qiyuwen yanjiu* 宋代 祈雨文研究 ("A Study of Song Dynasty Texts on Praying for Rain"). Northwest Normal University in China (2013. Available on-line at www. docin.com

Yoshikawa Kōjirō, see Watson, Burton.

Yü Chün-fang. *Kuan-yin: The Chinese Transformation of Avalokiteśvara.* New York: Columbia University Press, 2000.

Character List of Names and Terms

an 庵, "hermitage," a hut or retreat

Bai Juyi (Bo Juyi), also Bai Xiangshan 白居易, 白香山 (772–846) renowned Tang poet

baobian 褒貶 "praise-and-blame"

Bashi jing 八師經 (3rd c or earlier) *Sutra of the Eight Teachers*, translated by Zhiqian

Bi Hong 畢宏 (Tang dynasty) painter skilled at depicting pine trees

Chan 禪 Chinese rendering of *dhyāna,* Sanskrit term for "meditation" (Japanese: Zen)

Chen Tuan, also Xiyi 陳摶, 希夷 (fl. 920–989) Daoist sage and alchemist

Chu ci 楚辭, 楚詞 (4th c BC) *Songs of the State of Chu,* also *Songs of the South;* see Qu Yuan

Chun qiu 春秋 (6th c BC) *Spring and Autumn Annals,* composed by Confucius

Cui Bai 崔白 (fl. 1004–1088) Northern Song painter

Cui Kuang 崔鶠 (1015–1099), Boling man whose epitaph was composed by the poet Zhang Lei

Dao de jing 道德經 (3rd c BC?) *The Classic of the Way and its Power*

Dao Gai, also Maoguan 到溉, 茂灌 (477–548) Qi and Liang period writer

Daoyuan 道原 (10th c) monk, compiler of the *Jingde Chuandeng lu*

Deng Yin 鄧隱 (n.d.) early painter of Buddhist subjects

Duan Chengshi 段成式 (mid-9th century) poet and scholar; see *Youyang zazu*

Fajia 法家 "Legalist School," more precisely "School of Policy"

Fan Bailu 范百祿 (1030–1094) author of Wen Tong's tomb epitaph

Fan Chengda 范成大 (1126–1193) one of the "Four Masters" of Southern Song poetry

Fan Kuan 范寬 (fl. 990–1020) one of the supreme masters of Chinese painting

guqi 穀漆 "lacquer juice" (the character gu 谷 can substitute for gu 穀, "grain")

Han Yu 韓愈 (768–824) scholar and poet; see "Song Li Yuan gui Pangu xu"

He Shouwu lu 何首烏錄 (9th c) *A Record of Blackhead He,* essay by Li Ao on *Fallopia multiflora,* which he believed to be a magical herb

Hong Mai 洪邁 (1123–1202), Song dynasty historian and author of the *Yi Jian zhi*

Huailian 懷璉 (n.d.) noted monk and contemporary of Wen Tong

Huang Quan 黃筌 (903–965) master painter known for "bird and flower" paintings

Jia Chengzhi 家誠之 (fl. 12th c) editor of Wen Tong's works (colophon dated 1195)

Jia Dao 賈島 (793–865) sometime Buddhist monk and poet

Jiang Xu 蔣詡 famous recluse of the Han Dynasty

Jiao Guang 焦光 recluse of the late Han and a character in *Romance of the Three Kingdoms.*

jiao 醮 an important Daoist sacrificial rite

Jigu lu 集古錄 *A Record of Gathered Antiquities,* by Ouyang Xiu

jing, jingjie 境, 境界 "realm"

Jingde Chuandeng lu 景德傳燈錄 (1004) *Jingde Era* [1004–1007] *Record of the Transmission of the Lamp*), compiled by the monk Daoyuan

Jingxun 景遜 (n.d.) contemporary of Wen Tong

jinshi 進士 "presented scholar" degree

Jiu zhang suan shu 九章算術 (Former Han dynasty) *Mathematical Techniques in Nine Chapters*

Juna (1010–1071), 居訥 an associate of fellow-monk Huailian

ju 局 situations, as in a board game like *weiqi* chess

kaopan 考槃 "build a retreat" meaning to go into reclusion

Kong Zhigui 孔稚珪 (448–501) noted nature poet

kong 桯 "sounding-box" (music)

Li Ao, also Xizhi 李翱, 习之 (772–841) Tang philosopher and author of the *He Shouwu lu*

Li Cheng, also Yingqiu 李成, 營丘 (919-967) one of the supreme masters of Chinese painting

Li E 厲鶚 (1692–1752) scholar and editor, compiler of the *Songshi jishi*

Li He 李賀 (790–816) poet called the "ghostly genius"

Li Kan 李衎 (1245–1320) bamboo painter and author of the *Zhu pu*

Li Mengzhou, also Xiaozhen 李蒙州, 孝貞 official of the early Sui

Li Yangbing 李陽冰 (8th century) famous master of archaic "seal calligraphy"

Li Yu 李育 (1020–1069) Suzhou poet

li 理 "principle"

Liu Chang, also Yuanfu 劉敞, 原甫 (1019–1068) scholar and collector of antiquities

Liu Gongdu 柳公度 old man of the Tang dynasty whose healthy longevity was officially recorded

Liu Ling 劉伶 (221–300) eccentric Daoist recluse, poet, and famous drunkard

Liu Yunwen 劉允文 (n.d.) contemporary of Wen Tong famed for painting Buddhist subjects

Liu Yuxi 劉禹錫 (772–842) Tang poet dubbed a "hero of poetry"

Liu Zongyuan, also Zihou 柳宗元, 子厚 (773–819) scholar who wrote a poem on the herb *xianlingbi*

Lü Xiaqing, also Jinshu 呂夏卿, 縉叔 (1015/18–1070) scholar and editor

Mei Yaochen, also Shengyu 梅堯臣, 聖俞 (1002–1060) major poet of the Song dynasty

Meng Jiao, 孟郊 (751–814) famous poet of the mid-Tang Dynasty

Mijiao 密教 "Secret Teaching" or "Esoteric Buddhism"

Minxing, also Wuyan 敏行, 無演 Buddhist monk and contemporary of Wen Tong

muzhiming 墓誌銘 "tomb epitaph"

Ouyang Xiu 歐陽修 (1007–1072) scholar, statesman, and historian, author of the *Jigu lu*

Pan Yue 潘岳 (247–300) poet noted as well for his good looks

qi 錡 a stand for bows or spears

Qianfu lun 潛夫論 *Discourse on the Man Who's Hidden Away,* by Wang Fu

Qisong 契嵩 (1007–1072) noted monk

Qu Yuan 屈原 (fl. 340–278 BC) exiled statesman and poet, his works found in the *Chu Ci* anthology

Ruisheng Furen 睿聖夫人 "Lady of Sagacious Wisdom" honorific title for a local dragon goddess

Rujia 儒家, "School of the Scholars," i.e., Confucianism

ru 儒 (Confucian) scholars

san jiao 三教 the "Three Teachings," of Confucianism, Daoism, and Buddhism

Sengzhao 僧肇 (384–418) Buddhist monk and translator of Indian texts into Chinese

Shang Ziping 尚子平 a legendary hermit of antiquity

Shen Gua (Guo) 沈括 (1031–1095) Song dynasty polymath

Sheng'an shihua 升庵詩話 *Comments on Poetry from the Ascension Studio,* by Yang Shen

Shi ji 史記 *Records of the Historian,* by Sima Qian

Shiming (釋名) *Explication of Names,* an early dictionary dating from AD ca. 200

sigui 思歸 "yearning to return"

Sima Qian 司馬遷 (ca. 135 – 86 BC) Han dynasty historian and author of the *Shi ji*

Sima Xiangru 司馬相如 (179-117 BC) Han official and poet

Song Di, also Fugu 宋迪, 復古 (fl. 1015–1080?) painter and friend of Su Shi

Song Li Yuan gui Pangu xu 送李愿歸盤谷序 "Preface [and Poem on] Seeing Off Li Yuan on his Retirement to Pangu," by Han Yu

Song shi chao 宋詩鈔 (1671 with later addenda) *Volumes of Song Shi Poetry,* which included many of Wen Tong's poems; see Wu Zhizhen

Songshi jishi 宋詩紀事 (18th c?) *Recording Matters Pertaining to Song Poetry;* see Li E

Su Jun 蘇鈞 (n.d.) friend of Wen Tong

Su Shi, also Su Dongpo, or Zizhan 蘇軾, 蘇東坡, 子瞻 (1037–1101) generally regarded as the leading literatus and poet of the Song Dynasty.

Su Wen 蘇汶 (fl. earlier Song or Five Dynasties period) nothing further appears to be known of him

Su Zhe (Che) 蘇轍 (1039–1112) poet and younger brother of Su Shi

Su Ziping 蘇子平 (n.d.) name occurring in Wen's writings, possibly a pseudonym for Su Shi

Sun Taigu 孫太古 (n.d.) early painter of Buddhist subjects

Tangfushanyao 唐福山藥 "Tangfu Mountain herb," or "The herb of Mr. Tang Fushan."

Tao Yuanming, also Tao Qian 陶淵明, 陶潛 (365–427) recluse poet of the Six Dynasties period

Teng Changyou 滕昌佑 (10th c) painter of flowers

ti hulu 提葫蘆 "grab-a-gourd" or "grab-a-jug," name for the pelican

Tuhui baojian 圖繪寶鑑 (14th c) *The Precious Mirror of Painting* by Xia Wenyan

Wang Anshi 王安石 (1021–1086) Prime Minister and poet

Wang Fu 王符 (c 82–167 AD) philosopher and author of the *Discourse on the Man Who's Hidden Away*

Wang Guowei 王國維 (1877–1927) poet, critic, and scholar of Chinese vernacular literature

Wang Huizhi 王徽之 (d. 388), son of Wang Xizhi, exemplary literatus and lover of bamboo

Wang Xizhi 王羲之 (303–361), noted calligrapher who hosted the Spring Purification gathering at the Orchid Pavilion

Wei Yan 韋偃 (8th c) painter famed for his skill at depicting pine trees

Weizhong, also Huiya 惟中, 慧雅 (980–1045) Buddhist monk

wen 文 "text," a type of memorial to the throne

Wen Tong, also Yuke, or Huzhou 文同, 與可, 湖州 (1019–1079) scholar, poet, and master painter of bamboo

Wu Daozi 吳道子 (fl. 680–759) famous Tang painter

Wu Zhizhen 吳之振 (1640–1717) editor of the *Song shi chao*

wudong 烏鶇 blackbird

wuwei 無為 "doing nothing," "non-action"

Xi (Ji) Kang 嵇康 (223–262) recluse scholar, poet, and musician

xi 兮 "Ah!," "O!," "Yea!" a particle used as exclamation

Xia Wenyan 夏文彥 (1296–1370) Yuan scholar and author of the *Tuhui baojian*

xian 仙 an Immortal in Daoism

Xiang Yu, also Xiang Ji 項羽, 項籍 (232–202 BC) warlord of the late Qin dynasty

xianlingbi 仙靈毗 *Epimedium brevicornu* Maxim, herb believed to possess magical powers

Xianyu Shen, also Zijun 鮮于侁, 子駿 (1019-1087) poet and contemporary of Wen Tong

Xiao Yue 蕭悅 (fl. 800) credited as the first master of bamboo painting

Xu Daoning 許道寧 (fl. 970–1051/53) Northern Song master of landscape painting

Xue Ji 薛稷 (649–713) painting master known for "bird and flower" subjects

Yang Shen 楊慎 (1488–1559) Ming dynasty poet and scholar; see *Sheng'an shihua*

Yang Wanli 楊萬里 (1127–1206) one of the "Four Masters" of Southern Song poetry

Yangzhou 洋州 county in Shaanxi Province

Yi Jian zhi 夷堅志 *Matters Recorded by Master Yi Jian*, by Hong Mai

Yi jing 易經 *Book of Changes*

Yi Yuanji 易元吉 (fl. 1000–ca. 1064) famed painter of gibbons, deer, and other fauna

Yixing 一行 (683–727) Buddhist monk, mathematician, and calendrical expert

Youyang zazu 酉陽雜俎 *Miscellaneous Offerings on the Sacrificial Table from Youyang*, attributed (questionably) to Duan Chengshi

Yu Qing 虞卿 (n.d.) semi-legendary strategist of high antiquity

Zhang Jingru 張景孺 (n.d.) fellow official and friend of Wen Tong

Zhang Lei 張耒 (1052–1112) poet and friend and disciple of Su Shi

Zhao Li Si Feng Quji 詔李斯馮去疾 (fl. 226–209 BC) *Proclamation to Li Si and Feng Quji,* by the second Qin emperor

zhen 真 "truth"

Zhiqian 支謙 (d. ca. 252) translator of *Bashi jing*

Zhu pu 竹譜 (13th c) *Manual of Bamboo Painting;* see Li Kan

Zhuangzi 莊子 (4th c BC) Daoist philosopher and title of text attributed to him

zhujin 朱槿 red hibiscus

Zitong 梓潼 hometown of Wen Tong, present-day Yantingxian 鹽亭縣 in Sichuan Province

CAVE OF THE IMMORTALS
THE POETRY AND PROSE OF BAMBOO PAINTER
WEN TONG (1019–1079)

 In the history of Chinese art, Wen Tong (1019–1079) is considered the supreme master of bamboo painting. This widely shared assessment has perhaps overshadowed his equally brilliant poetry, which has remained virtually unknown. This book is the first in any Western language to present translations of selected poetry and prose by Wen, writings that bring to light aspects of Buddhism, Daoism, and Confucianism rarely addressed by Chinese poets, as they involve devotional practices held in suspicion by many literati. A particular revelation is Wen's unusual interest in what might be called the folk religion of China, including tales of strange and supernatural events, and ceremonies of supplication to various gods, especially dragon deities controlling the rain.

Jonathan Chaves is a professor of Chinese language and literature at The George Washington University, and a published original poet. He has been awarded the Lucien Stryk Prize for best translation from an Asian work of literature, conferred by the American Literary Translators Association, and the Japan-U.S. Friendship Commission Prize for best translation, and has been nominated for the National Book Award in Translation.

Floating World Editions

Floating World Editions publishes books that contribute to a deeper understanding of Asian cultures. Editorial supervision: Ray Furse. Book and cover design: Michelle Landry, Digital Dragon Designery. Printing and binding: IngramSpark. The typefaces used are Adobe Garamond Pro, Trajan Pro, Droid Serif, Source Sans Pro, and SimSun.

CPSIA information can be obtained
at www.ICGtesting.com
Printed in the USA
BVHW072324230822
645258BV00002BA/6

9 781891 640902